The Way We Were
RIDING THE RAILS

The Way We Were

RIDING THE RAILS

MICHAEL SWIFT

CHARTWELL
BOOKS, INC.

This edition published by:

CHARTWELL BOOKS, INC.
A Division of
BOOK SALES, INC.
114 Northfield Avenue
Edison, New Jersey 08837

ISBN 13: 978-0-7858-2444-2
ISBN 10: 0-7858-2444-8

2008 by Compendium Publishing Ltd.
43 Frith Street, London W1D 4SA,
United Kingdom

Cataloging-in-publication data is available from the Library of Congress.

Designer: Dave Ball
Color reproduction: Anorax
Printed in: China

PAGE 1: Railroad publicity posters and brochures of the 1920s and 1930s were as stylish as the stock. This is the CB&Q's brochure launching the "Burlington Zephyr." *Ian Allan Library*

PAGES 2–3: America is big, and the railroads were the perfect 19th century answer to long-distance transportation of people, livestock, raw materials, manufactured goods — just about everything. The arrival of the aircraft and automobile dented this preeminence sev erely, but with global warming, increased fuel prices, and other 21st century considerations, the time could be right for a revival. *Ian Allan Library*

RIGHT: At the end of World War II there were some 37,500 steam locomotives in service on U.S. railroads; just over a decade later most had been consigned for scrap as the railroads made a dash for diesel or electric traction. Northern Pacific Class A-3 4-8-4 No. 2661 could accommodate 27 tons of coal and 20,000 gallons of water in its tender. *Ian Allan Library*

CONTENTS

INTRODUCTION

The dawn of the railroad age occurred in the early years of the Industrial Revolution and was equally important for the development of the modern economy and society. Railroads permitted the growth of industry by allowing for the cheap movement of both raw materials and finished goods, and the growth of urban society, by facilitating the shipment of the goods and services essential for the viability of cities. Railroads also fostered, as far as the United States of America is concerned, the growth of the nation; indeed the growth of the Union in the 19th century would perhaps have been impossible without the development of the transcontinental railroad routes after the Civil War.

Although much of the pioneering work in the development of railroads occurred in Europe, in particular in Britain during the first three decades of the 19th century, it was not long before the technology associated with railroad construction and operation crossed the Atlantic and the first pioneering railroads were completed in the U.S.A.

It is generally accepted that the first public railroad in the U.S.A. was the Baltimore & Ohio, which was first launched at a meeting of Baltimore businessmen in 1827, only two years after the opening of the pioneering Stockton and Darlington Railway in Britain, and three years before the equally important Liverpool and Manchester. (Although there were earlier lines, such as the Granite Railway at Quincy, in Boston, constructed in 1826 for work on the Bunker Hill memorial, these were not "public" in the sense of offering a public service.) Despite opposition from powerful forces including Congress, work started on July 4, 1828 and the first 13-mile section opened in May 1830. Initially horse-powered, the line received its first steam locomotive in August 1830, Peter Cooper's Tom Thumb. However, this locomotive was not the first in the U.S.A. That honor belonged to an imported locomotive from Britain — the

BELOW: The construction of the Baltimore and Ohio (B&O) required the erection of a major viaduct at Relay, Maryland. Opened in July 4, 1835, the structure is the oldest stone-arch railway viaduct in the world. This contemporary view, published in Britain, shows a steam train crossing the bridge. *Ian Allan Library*

Stourbridge Lion — which had been tested on the Delaware & Hudson Canal & Railroad, but which had been deemed unsuitable by the company's engineer, Horatio Allen.

During these early years a number of steam locomotives were imported from Britain and these designs — in particular the 4-4-0 developed by Edward Bury and exported to the U.S.A. by his company Bury, Curtis and Kennedy — were to influence early U.S. locomotive development. Given the availability of vast quantities of wood, most early U.S. steam locomotives were designed to be wood-fired, rather than coal which was preferred in Europe. This factor also affected the development of U.S. steam locomotives when coal was gradually adopted as an alternative. Unfortunately, the most readily available coal had a high anthracite content, which proved difficult to burn in the small fireboxes of the day. This problem resulted in some of the more unusual designs to emerge during these early years. The early coal-burning locomotives were fitted with vertical, as opposed to the more usual horizontal boilers; as a result of their peculiar shape and motion, these locomotives were nicknamed "Grasshoppers" or "Crabs". They were slow in operation and therefore further action was required. Ross Winans developed an alternative design, with an enlarged firebox and with the cab

LEFT: U.S. Military Railroad engine *W.H. Whiton*, and the president's rail car, later used as Lincoln's funeral car. *Library of Congress*

RIGHT: Competition on the railroads could be cut-throat; this contemporary cartoon portrays Commodore Cornelius Vanderbilt of the New York Central Railroad — one of the more controversial railroad entrepreneurs of the period — competing with the Erie Railroad for traffic to the west of New York. The Erie Railroad was one of those that suffered financial failure during the late 19th century. *Library of Congress*

FAR RIGHT: One of the most famous incidents involving the railroads during the Civil War was the seizure of the locomotive, *The General* by soldiers of the Union Army in April 1862. They then proceeded to drive the engine from Marietta, Georgia, to Chattanooga. It was this incident that inspired the classic Buster Keaton film *The General*. *Bettmann/Corbis BE038567*

BELOW RIGHT: A closer look at the president's rail car, later used as Lincoln's funeral car. *Library of Congress*

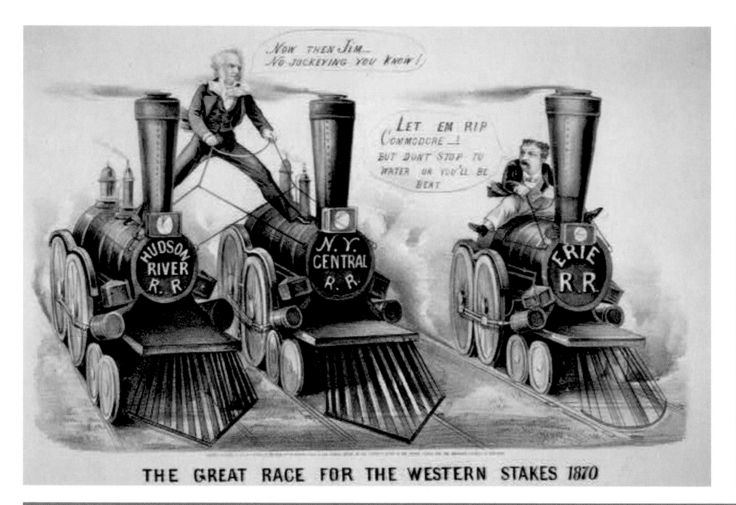

THE GREAT RACE FOR THE WESTERN STAKES 1870

"Railroads are the weakest things in war. A single man with a match can destroy and cut off communications."

Sherman

located above the boiler; these locomotives, nicknamed for obvious reasons "Camels," first appeared in 1848 and this design was to be further refined later in the 19th century as "Camelbacks" (or "Mother Hubbards").

Between the early 1830s and the outbreak of the Civil War in 1861, the railroad network of the U.S.A. expanded rapidly: during the 1850s the total route mileage trebled, to some 30,000 miles by the end of the decade. Railroads were still largely an East coast phenomenon, but the discovery of gold in California provided the necessary incentive to drive development ever westwards. The 1850s witnessed the construction of a number of highly significant routes, including the westward extensions of the New York Central and Erie railroads to Lake Erie, and extensions of the Baltimore & Ohio (B&O) and Pennsylvania up the Ohio Valley. Although many of the lines constructed were built to the accepted standard gauge of 4 ft 8½ in., this was not uniform. The Lake Erie, for example, was constructed to a gauge of 6 ft 0 in. and many of the lines in Ohio were built to a gauge of 4 ft 10 inches. While the network was relatively fragmented, this did not prove a serious handicap, but once problems of transhipment and interchange of rolling stock occurred, the differences in gauge proved a barrier. It was not until the 1880s that

4 ft 8½ in. became the accepted national standard; the last southern routes were converted on June 1, 1886.

Although there had been rapid development of the railway infrastructure up to 1860, the onset of the Civil War in 1861 was to lead to both damage to existing lines and delays to new projects. The American Civil War was the first major conflict in the world in which the railroads played an influential role. Both sides used them to move significant quantities of men and equipment, and both attacked railroads in enemy territory as a means of disrupting their communication. As a result, by the cessation of hostilities in 1865, much damage had been wrought to the railroad infrastructure of the country and it took some time for this to be repaired.

The next 50 years were to see further massive development in the country's railroad network, symbolized perhaps, by that moment on May 10, 1869 when the golden spike was inserted at Promontory Point, Utah, between the Union Pacific and Central Pacific railroads to mark the completion of the first transcontinental railroad. During these 50 years not all developments were positive, however. The railroad industry was tainted with accusations of corruption, financial chicanery, unfair competition and profiteering.

THE COMING OF THE RAILWAYS

Although the Baltimore & Ohio, which opened in May 1830, is generally regarded as the first true railroad in the U.S.A., the first successful steam-operated railroad in the U.S.A. was probably the South Carolina Railroad, which inaugurated its services on December 25, 1830, using the vertical-boilered *Best Friend* of Charleston. At this date there were only some 23 miles of operational railroad track in the U.S.A., 13 miles of which was represented by the Baltimore & Ohio. However, once the principal of the steam-hauled railway was established, expansion was rapid. Within five years of the opening of the B&O, total track mileage in the U.S.A. reached more than 1,000 miles and this total almost trebled by 1840, when some 2,800 route miles were in operation. By the end of the 1840s, 9,000 miles of route had been constructed, although the bulk — about two-thirds — was located in eleven East Coast states (New York, with some 1,361 route miles possessed the most intensive network in 1850). By the eve of the Civil War,

the iron network in the United States was more than 30,000 miles long, and the railroads of the western lines had nearly caught up with the ever-advancing western frontier. Following the Civil War, several lines were extended all the way to the Pacific coast, the first being the Union Pacific–Central Pacific, completed in 1869. By 1890 the length of the U.S. rail system was 163,000 miles; by 1916 it had reached an all-time high of 254,000 miles.

WASON MANUFACTURING COMPANY OF SPRINGFIELD, MASS.
RAILWAY CAR BUILDERS.
CAR WHEELS AND GENERAL RAILWAY WORK.

FAR LEFT: In order to support the expanding railroad industry, a vast array of new factories grew up to construct locomotives, wagons, passenger cars, and the entire infrastructure associated with the needs of the burgeoning business. This late 19th century photograph portrays the works at Springfield, Massachusetts, of the Wason Manufacturing Co. *Library of Congress*

LEFT: Built by the West Point Foundry in New York, *De Witt Clinton* first operated over the South Carolina Railroad on August 9, 1831. It survived to appear at the Chicago World's Fair Exhibition of 1893. *Ian Allan Library*

LEFT: Chinese laborers at work with picks, shovels, wheelbarrows, and one-horse carts on the long trestle bridge that was originally built in 1865 on the present Southern Pacific Railroad lines at Sacramento. The picture was taken in 1877 and shows the crude construction methods in use when the first railroad was built across the Sierra Nevada Mountains. *Bettmann/Corbis U362099INP*

BELOW: As the railroad network expanded, so the promoters faced the challenge of crossing ever-wider rivers and penetrating further into the nation's vast mountain ranges. This is a view of the Kansas City & Memphis Railway's bridge across the Mississippi at Memphis, Tennessee, taken during the early years of the 20th century. *Library of Congress*

BOTTOM: The coming of the railroads opened up the country and enabled the massive growth of the economy. This image shows the scale of the Great Union Stock Yards in Chicago in 1878. The railroad yards served no fewer than 37 packhouses and numerous slaughterhouses and other facilities. It was only the railroad that could provide a cost-effective and efficient means of moving large quantities of livestock and other products nationwide. *Library of Congress*

THE GREAT UNION STOCK YARDS OF CHICAGO.

BUILDING THE RAILWAYS

In an era before mechanized construction, the building of railroads required a vast manpower. Cuttings, tunnels, embankments, and bridges all had to be built and all required significant labor. While routes could be constructed to follow the natural contour of the land, in order to minimize expense and labor requirements, physical structures were required when river crossings or mountain ranges blocked the route. The first multi-arched stone-built viaduct in the world was constructed for the Baltimore & Ohio Railroad, opening in 1835, the first of many spectacular structures erected during the golden age of the railroads. Many lines were constructed alongside river valleys, again to help minimize construction costs, although this did result in many U.S. railroads being prone to washouts when the rivers flooded, and a number of lines ultimately closed as a result of flood damage. Another means of efficient construction was the use of easily accessible materials; thus, there was considerable use of timber in the construction of railroad bridges, unlike in Europe, where iron or steel were preferred. Finally, particularly when work started on the transcontinental routes, there was always the potential threat from hostile Native American tribes.

ABOVE: With the formation completed and the sleepers embedded, all that is required now is for the track to be laid. *Library of Congress*

RIGHT: A contemporary line drawing illustrating the construction of railroad across the Great Plains. Although everything would appear to be peaceful in this view, the presence of the armed soldiers in the foreground emphasizes the potent threat posed by the local Native Americans. *Library of Congress*

RIGHT: In an age before mechanized construction, the building of a railroad required considerable manpower. Here, the shovel is the most advanced piece of equipment available to these workers as they construct a junction at Devereux station on the Chicago & Alexandria Railroad. *Library of Congress*

RIGHT: The use of easily accessible materials — most notably timber — was a means by which construction could be quickly and cheaply effected. Wooden bridges, however, required regular repair and were prone to being washed away when inundated with floodwater. *Library of Congress*

BELOW: The new railroad bridge across the Susquehanna from Havre le Grace to Perryville, Maryland, 1866. *Library of Congress*

FAR RIGHT: Even in the first years of the 20th century, the construction of railroads was still labor-intensive; here workers move by hand sections of track as they lay the first rails in Ship Creek, Alaska. *Library of Congress*

D–SHIP CREEK

THE CIVIL WAR

The early years of the 1860s witnessed the first major war in the world in which the railroad played a significant part. Both the Confederate and Union forces made considerable use of railroads for the movement of men and materiel; in the autumn of 1863, for example, 30,000 Union troops were moved by rail in order to help relieve Chattanooga in Tennessee, which was then under Confederate siege. The railroads meant that armies could move men and equipment much more quickly and in much greater quantities than before. As both sides realized the potential of the railroads, they also realized that destroying the enemy's lines of communication would aid their own campaign and the war was thus to witness considerable destruction. By the end of the war, the country's railroads were near to collapse, but it would not be long before they were restored and expansion could continue apace.

LEFT: The Richmond & Petersburg Railroad station in Richmond, Virginia, photographed in 1865 shows the damage wrought during the Civil War. *Library of Congress*

BELOW: As recorded in a contemporary journal, this portrays the capture of a train at Magnolia on the Philadelphia, Wilmington & Baltimore Railroad on July 11, 1864, during the invasion of Maryland. *Library of Congress*

RIGHT: Military railroad operations in Virginia around 1863. *Library of Congress*

LEFT: Military railroad operations in Virginia around 1863. *Library of Congress*

ABOVE: During the late autumn of 1864 Sherman occupied Atlanta, Georgia, and before his army retreated they wrought much destruction on the railroad infrastructure of the city. This view, taken towards the end of the occupation, shows the railroad depot having been blown up by Sherman's troops. *Library of Congress*

RIGHT: During Grant's campaign south of the James River in Virginia, reinforcements for General Warren are brought by train to the terminus of Grant's railroad near the Weldon Road in late 1864. The scene was illustrated here in Frank Leslie's *Illustrated Newspaper* of October 22, 1864. *Library of Congress*

BELOW RIGHT: The American Civil War was the first conflict in history where the railroads played a significant role. Here a rudimentary rail-borne howitzer is pictured with cannon balls ready to fire. *Corbis IH079557*

FAR RIGHT: Members of the U.S. Military Railroad Construction Corps repair the track of the Orange & Alexandria Railroad in Virginia, c.1863. This railroad was used as a supply line by both the Confederate and Union armies. *Library of Congress*

UNITING THE NATION

Following the declaration of peace in 1865 and the restoration of the wartime damage, there was a massive development in the country's railroad infrastructure. On May 10, 1869, the first transcontinental railroad was completed when the golden spike was inserted at Promontory Point, Utah, where the Union Pacific met the Central Pacific railroad. Between 1870 and the turn of the century, a further four routes would be completed across the continent: the Southern Pacific from California to New Orleans; the Santa Fe from Kansas to California; the Northern Pacific from Minnesota to Seattle; and the Great Northern. Between 1865, when the Civil War concluded, and 1916, on the eve of the U.S.A.'s entry into World War 1, total route mileage in the country increased from some 30,000 miles to a massive 254,000 miles.

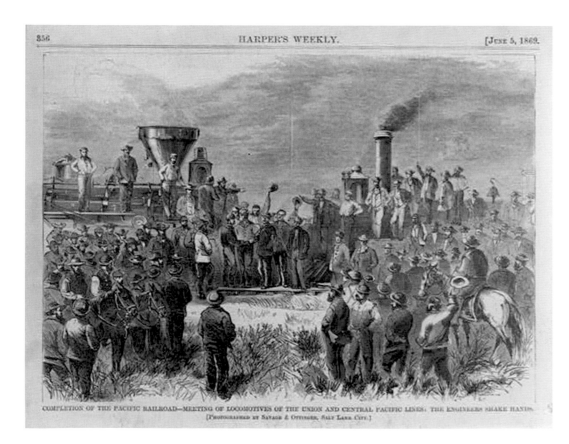

COMPLETION OF THE PACIFIC RAILROAD—MEETING OF LOCOMOTIVES OF THE UNION AND CENTRAL PACIFIC LINES: THE ENGINEERS SHAKE HANDS.
[PHOTOGRAPHED BY SAVAGE & OTTINGER, SALT LAKE CITY.]

LEFT: The *Harper's Weekly* report of June 5, 1869 recording the meeting of the Union and Central Pacific railroads. *Library of Congress*

RIGHT: Giant Bluff on the Elk Canyon, Black Hills & Fort Pierre Railroad in South Dakota recorded in 1890. Theoretically, following the Treaty of Fort Laramie of 1868, the Black Hills were recognized as Native American territory; however, in 1874 General Custer led an illegal expedition into the territory, proving that gold was present. The result was inevitable and, reflecting the opening up of the region, work started in 1881 on the construction of the ECBH&SPR. The last sections of this narrow gauge railroad closed in 1930. Elsewhere in the USA — such as in California and Alaska — the discovery of gold or other minerals provided a considerable stimulus to the development of the railroad network. *Library of Congress*

No. 3572. "Giant Bluff."
Elk Canyon on Black Hills & Ft. P.
R. R.
Photo and Copyright by Grabill, '90
Deadwood and Lead City, S. D.

PULLMAN

Founded in the 1860s by George Pullman, whose experience of traveling by an overnight train from Buffalo to Westfield, New York, had encouraged him to design a new passenger car, the Pullman Palace Car Company was one of a number — but undoubtedly the best known — of companies that sought to promote railroads as a means of luxury travel. The company manufactured cars for a number of railroads both in the United States and overseas, reaching its peak in the mid-1920s when its fleet numbered 9,800 cars and it employed some 40,000 conductors and porters. However, in the early 1940s, the U.S. Department of Justice took anti-trust action against the company, ultimately forcing its break-up. The name of "Pullman" disappeared at the end of December 1968 when all the remaining operational leases were terminated, although the company remained a manufacturer thereafter, building rolling stock until the 1980s and its railway design business eventually passed to Bombardier. There is still a company using the Pullman in part, which can trace its ancestry back to the original company founded by George Pullman, although it no longer has any involvement in the railroad business.

FAR LEFT: A poster from 1894 promoting the Pullman service of the Cincinnati, Hamilton & Dayton Railroad. *Library of Congress*

LEFT: The interior of a 19th century Pullman car as depicted at the end of the century. *Bettmann/Corbis E3346*

BELOW: In March 1942 a porter makes up an upper berth on the "Capital Ltd" service for Chicago. *Library of Congress*

RIGHT: The interior of the Santa Barbara, which was constructed for the Southern Pacific Railroad in 1887. The interior of the car, which had a wooden body, was finished in mahogany, English oak, and satin-wood. *Bettmann/Corbis BE039388*

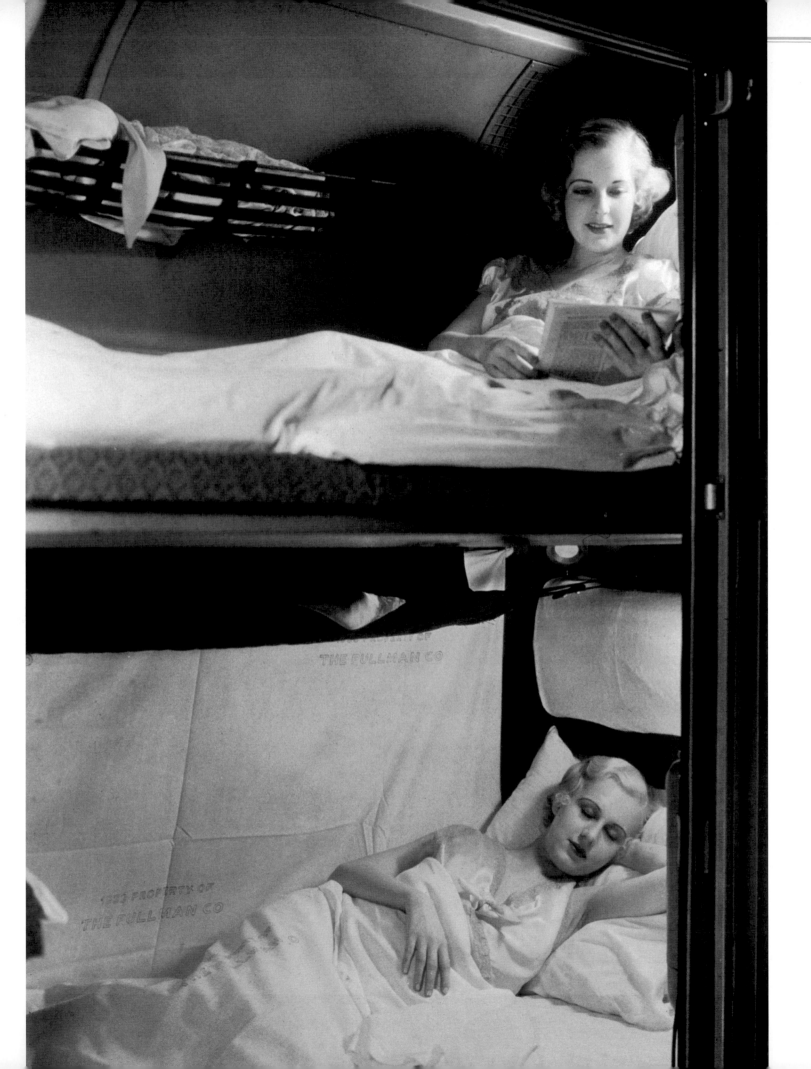

THE GREAT RAILROADS

Atchison, Topeka & Santa Fe

Known generally as the Santa Fe, construction of the AT&SFR started at Topeka, Kansas, in 1872 and by 1887 had reached Los Angeles. Later extensions saw the company extend to Oakland, on San Francisco Bay, and Galveston in Texas. For a brief period in the early 20th century the Santa Fe was merged with the St Louis & San Francisco Railroad, but this was soon reversed. The AT&SFR extends over some 12,000 route miles and, like most U.S. railroads, is predominantly a carrier of heavy freight over long distances. The company used steam until 1959 but was a pioneer in the use of diesel traction, acquiring its first locomotives in 1935. The company merged with the Burlington Northern in 1995 to become Burlington Northern Santa Fe (BNSF).

LEFT: Locomotives of the Atchison, Topeka & Santa Fe Railroad are serviced at the Argentine Yard in Kansas, during March 1943. Closest to the camera is No. 4000. *Library of Congress*

TOP RIGHT: A westbound Santa Fe freight train stands at signals at Ricardo, New Mexico, in March 1943 awaiting clearance to enter the next section. *Library of Congress*

RIGHT: The "3765" class of 4-8-4 was the largest class of locomotive built for passenger service on the Atchison, Topeka & Santa Fe Railroad. Although the class was oil-fired, the type was designed to be converted to coal-burning if required. The first of the class of 11 was built in 1938 by Baldwin in 1936; one of the type, No 3768, survives in preservation. *Ian Allan Library*

ABOVE: In 1928, the Baltimore & Ohio Railroad held an exhibition and pageant to mark the centenary of the line. Among the exhibits was an example of Ross Winan's design of "Camelback" locomotive. No. 217 was one of 119 locomotives of the type operated by the B&O and dated originally from 1873. The development of Winan's design from the 1840s was the result of the need to utilize a much larger firebox when using coal rather than the more usual timber. The locomotive is now preserved in the B&O Museum in Baltimore. *B&OR*

TOP RIGHT: Crowds wait to board two Baltimore & Ohio Budd-built Rail Diesel Cars (RDCs) at Cleveland in 1961; the RDCs, introduced by Budd in 1949, were designed to reduce the cost of operating passenger services and could operate singly or in multiple. *Harry Luff Collection/Online Transport Archive*

RIGHT: No. 5600 *George H. Emerson* was the first of the Baltimore & Ohio Railroad's 4-4-4-4 locomotives and was delivered in June 1936. The locomotive was designed to permit the boiler to generate pressure of 350 lb to each of the four cylinders. *Ian Allan Library*

Baltimore & Ohio

Generally accepted as the first railroad in the U.S.A. to build a line for general traffic, construction of the B&O commenced in July 4, 1828, and the first 13 miles from Baltimore to Ellicott Mills opened using horse power in May 1830. On August 1830 steam first appeared and over the following years the line was gradually extended, reaching Cumberland, 178 miles from Baltimore, in 1842. The next section, through the Allegheny Mountains, took 11 years to complete, but the line opened through to Wheeling, West Virginia, on January 1, 1853. During the 1860s, the B&O was to suffer significant damage as a result of the American Civil War, but with peace restored in 1865, expansion continued. The B&O retained its independence until the 1970s when it became part of the Chessie System (later CSX Transportation).

RIGHT: Boston & Maine 2-8-0 No. 2394 was a "K6" class dating from 1935. The locomotive is pictured at the head of a local passenger train. *Ivan W. Saunders*

BELOW: A B&M commuter train leaves Boston for a run to South Acton in early 1976. Suburban services were, by this date, the only passenger services operated by the B&M and were subsidized by the Massachusetts Bay Transportation Authority. *Brian J. Cudahy*

Boston & Maine

The Boston & Maine Railroad is the largest railroad operator in New England and represents the merger of some 100 smaller companies, the earliest of which — the Andover & Wilmington — was opened in 1836 and linked the states of Massachusetts and Maine. At its peak in the early 1920s, the B&MR possessed 2,248 miles of route. The company constructed the 4¾-mile long Hoosac Tunnel between Greenfield and upstate New York, with work being completed in 1876; this was the longest tunnel in the U.S.A. when built, and remains in use today. When the B&MR was predominantly steam-operated, locomotives were piloted through the tunnel by electric locomotives to avoid steam and smoke polluting the tunnel. Although the company still operates some commuter services into its Boston North station, the remainder of its work is freight only. The B&M merged with Maine Central and later with the Delaware & Hudson to form the Guilford System in 1984.

ABOVE: Hoosac Tunnel publicity. *Corbis IH196004*

RIGHT: EMD "F7A" No. 4266 of the Boston & Maine Railroad is now preserved at the Conway Scenic Railroad. *Brian Solomon*

"Today a new transcontinental line, the Chicago, Milwaukee, St Paul and Chicago, Milwaukee & Puget Sound Railways, opening boundless resources still untouched in the magnificent region discovered, testifies to the enduring work of the Pioneer."
CMStP&PR 1912

Chicago, Milwaukee, St Paul & Pacific

The first section of the future CMSP&P opened in 1851 as the Milwaukee & Waukesha Railroad, and by 1863 a total of 830 route miles was in operation. The line reached Chicago in 1873. A total of 6,000 route miles was in use by 1900, with the company's routes extending as far as Kansas. The Pacific Ocean itself was reached in 1909 and was incorporated into the company's title in 1913. Competition resulted in financial problems for the CMSP&P from the 1960s, which were exacerbated by the rejection of a proposed merger with the C&NW. The company went bankrupt for the third time in December 1977 and, as a result, the Pacific extension was abandoned in 1980, although this later re-emerged as a smaller, regional company. Despite the restructuring, the CMSP&P continued to struggle and was taken over by Soo Line in February 1985.

FAR LEFT: The "Olympian Hiawatha" was one of the Chicago, Milwaukee, St Paul, & Pacific Railroad's most important services and, in 1947, the service was provided with new streamlined coaches, including the stylish "Skytop Lounge" observation cars seen here. *Harry Luff Collection/© Online Transport Archive*

LEFT: Recorded as Lackawanna Railroad No. 1661 at Waukesha, Wisconsin, on October 11, 1994, this 4-8-4 is actually Chicago, Milwaukee, St Paul, & Pacific Railroad No. 261. The CMSP&PR acquired 52 4-8-4s between 1930 and 1944; the last 10, designated Class S3, were built by Alco and delivered in 1944. All were withdrawn between 1954 and 1956 and two examples, including No. 261, were preserved. No. 261 is currently preserved in an operational condition at the National Railroad Museum, Ashwaubenon, Wisconsin. Sister locomotive No. 265 is preserved at the Illinois Railway Museum. *Brian Solomon*

ABOVE RIGHT: The Chicago & North Western Railroad acquired nine oil-burning "Hudson" type locomotives from Alco in 1938. Classified E-4 by the C&NW, the locomotives were numbered 4000–4008 and were constructed, as shown here by No. 4002, as streamliners. The locomotives were designed to haul the railroad's famous "400" express passenger services. However, even as the class was being delivered, the railroad decided that the future lay in diesel operation and the "E-4" class was rapidly transferred to other duties. The class was withdrawn from service by 1953 and none survive in preservation. *Ian Allan Library*

RIGHT:

Chicago & North Western

The Galena & Chicago Union Railroad, a constituent of the C&NW, was the first railway to the west of Chicago when it opened in October 1848. The C&NW itself was established in 1859 and by 1900 operated over some 8,300 route miles, which had increased by the late 1970s to 10,000 miles. The C&NW was to remain independent until 1988, one of the last of the great railroading names to survive, when it became part of the expanded Union Pacific.

BOTTOM: In 1930, the Delaware & Hudson introduced a class of high-pressure 2-8-0s similar to No. 1401 illustrated here. The locomotives were designed to operate with a boiler pressure of 500lb. *Ian Allan Library*

FAR RIGHT: Delaware & Hudson 4-6-6-4 No. 1500 is pictured hauling a freight. *Ian Allan Library*

Delaware & Hudson

The first U.S. railroad to operate steam locomotives regularly, the Delaware & Hudson, a railroad company that had its origins in a canal that opened in October 1828, survived for more than 150 years before becoming part of Guilford System in 1984. The company's first involvement with railroads came with the construction of a line from Carbondale to carry anthracite to the canal. The line was authorized in 1826 and, on August 8, 1829, the company's first steam locomotive—the British-built *Stourbridge Lion*—became the first steam locomotive to operate in the U.S. Further extensions to the railroad were built and the original canal gradually declined in importance; it was not to close finally until the 1890s and in 1899 the D&W dropped the word canal from its name. The railroad grew rapidly through acquisition during the last years of the 19th century and the first decades of the 20th. However, as with a number of other railroads, the company's finances deteriorated and, during the late 1960s and 1970s, underwent several reorganizations before the entire operation was taken over for $500,000 by Guilford Rail System as part of a scheme to create a regional railroad. Guilford sold the company in 1988 and in 1990 it became a subsidiary of Canadian Pacific.

FAR LEFT: A 4-6-6-4 articulated locomotive built for use on the Denver & Rio Grande Western Railroad. *D&RGWR*

LEFT: "K36" class No 480, built by Baldwin in 1925, is pictured about to depart from Maysville for Monarch on a train of empty gondolas on the narrow-gauge Denver & Rio Grande prior to the line's preservation. *Ian Allan Library*

BELOW: No. 1604 was a 4-8-2 belonging to Denver & Rio Grande Western after the bulk of the company's lines had been converted to standard gauge. *Ian Allan Library*

Denver & Rio Grande

Faced by the challenge of traversing the Rocky Mountains of Colorado, ex-Confederate General William Jackson Palmer adopted the 3 ft 0 in. gauge for construction of his line south from Denver. Work started at Denver in 1871 heading southwards, and by 1872 had reached Pueblo, where Palmer established the Central Colorado Improvement Co., a company which reorganized a decade later and was to provide the bulk of the line's traffic until the mid-1950s. In 1873 financial troubles led to delays and, by the time that Palmer was able to restart, the most obvious route to the south — the Raton Pass — had already been occupied by another railroad. Palmer then decided to head west in 1878, reaching Alamosa via the Sangre de Cristo Range and Veta Pass, but again the line's path was blocked by another company's line. In 1879 the courts ruled in favor of the Rio Grande, but the railway collapsed financially and the line came under the influence of Jay Gould, who also controlled the Union Pacific. Under Gould's guidance a settlement was reached which allowed the Rio Grande to expand further. However, as the line expanded, Gould's influence declined and Palmer regained control. In the 1880s, Palmer decided to convert the principal Rio Grande routes to standard gauge, resulting in the gradual decline of the remaining narrow gauge lines that led ultimately to closure, although sections have been reopened as tourist lines. As a standard gauge railway, the Rio Grande continued to grow. In 1920, when the line was sold, it became the Denver & Rio Grande Western; it merged with the Denver & Salt Lake in 1947 and, in 1988, the line was merged with the Southern Pacific when the D&RGW name was dropped.

Great Northern

Driven by the ambition of one man, James Jerome Hill, the GNR was constructed to the north of the Northern Pacific. The line was completed on September 18, 1893, and included the 7¾-mile long Cascade Tunnel, which became the longest tunnel on a U.S. railroad. The line through Cascade Tunnel was electrified in 1909 and replaced by 11.5 kV in 1927. A longer Cascade Tunnel was opened two years later. The electrified section was ultimately converted to diesel traction. The GNR became part of the Burlington Northern in 1970 and in 1995, part of the Burlington Northern Santa Fe.

FAR LEFT: Great Northern 4-8-2 No 2515. *Ian Allan Library*

ABOVE: The 4-8-4 was a logical development of the earlier 4-8-2 and 4-6-4 designs, as it allowed for a combination of the former's increased traction, as a result of more weight on the driving wheels, with the latter's enlarged firebox. The first 4-8-4 was delivered in January 1927 by ALCO for Northern Pacific. The type was operated by 32 U.S. railroads and was well suited for fast passenger and express freight services, with 927 units built for operation, including Great Northern No. 2552 illustrated here. *Ian Allan Library*

LEFT: Great Northern box car logo. *Time Life Pictures/Getty Images*

New York Central

The oldest section of the future New York Central was the Mohawk & Hudson Railroad between Albany and Schenectady, which was incorporated in 1826 and opened five years later. The name "New York Central" first appeared in 1853. Amongst lines that were ultimately to form part of the company were the New York Central & Hudson River, and the Lake Shore & Michigan railroads. One of the line's most famous locomotives, No. 999, built for the Chicago World's Fair of 1893, achieved a speed of 112 mph over a measured mile — a record which was to survive for many years The New York Central merged with the Pennsylvania Railroad in 1968 to become Penn Central. It was then subsumed in 1976 into Conrail.

RIGHT: "Rockefeller Center New York" — designed by Leslie Ragan, a poster promoting New York Central. *LLC/Corbis AAED002633*

CENTER: In April 1943, New York Central switcher No. 622 is seen in operation at the South Water Street freight depot in Chicago; the New York Central was one of a number of railroads that leased the yard. *Library of Congress*

FAR RIGHT: The "20th Century Limited" was one of the New York Central's mosty prestigious passenger services. *Ian Allan Library*

Norfolk & Western

The Norfolk & Western had its origins in the City Point Railroad, which opened out of Petersburg, Virginia, on 7 September 1838. Other earlier constituents included the Norfolk & Petersburg Railway, the Southside Railroad and the Virginia & Tennessee Railroad. The company became known as the Atlantic, Mississippi, & Ohio Railroad, before becoming the Norfolk & Western in 1881. Unlike other U.S. railroads, the N&W persisted with steam traction for longer; indeed the N&W used the last new steam locomotive constructed for use on a U.S. railroad, No. 244, entered service in 1953. But the N&W could not hold out against the trend and, on April 4, 1960, it ran its last steam-hauled service. In the mid-1950s the N&W extended over some 2,100 miles; over the next 20 years it was to expand rapidly through acquiring other railroads, reaching a total mileage of 7,500 miles by 1975. Among the companies it obtained were the Virginian Railroad in 1959 and the New York, Chicago, & St Louis in 1964. In 1982 N&W merged with Southern Railway to form Norfolk Southern, which then acquired a significant part of Conrail in 1999.

Class J 4-8-4 No. 600 of the Norfolk & Western; this class was the last design of steam locomotive specifically for express passenger service to be produced in the U.S. The first of the class was built at the railroad's Roanoke, Virginia, workshops, being completed in early 1941 and, ultimately, a total of 14 were built between then and 1950; when the last to be completed, No. 613, was finished in 1950 it became the last new steam passenger locomotive built in the U.S.A. Highly successful in service, the class operated some 80 percent of the railroad's passenger services until supplanted later in the 1950s. One of the class survives in preservation.

RIGHT: Norfolk & Western 0-8-0 No. 277 was standard switcher operated by the railroad. *Thomas T. Taber*

FAR RIGHT: Norfolk & Western Class A 2-6-6-4 No. 1200. This class of 43 locomotives built between 1936 and 1950 was the last type of 2-6-6-4 constructed for use on a U.S. railroad and also the most powerful. One of the class, No. 1218, survives in the Virginia Museum of Transportation, based at Roanoke, Virginia. *Ian Allan Library*

Pennsylvania

The origins of the Pennsylvania Railroad date back to November 12, 1831, with the opening of the Camden & Amboy Railroad in New Jersey. Initially steam-operated, the line's first engine was named John Bull; appropriately the locomotive had been built in England and shipped across the Atlantic. The "Pennsy", as the company was nicknamed, got its own charter in 1846 for the construction of the line between Pittsburgh and Philadelphia. Serving eight of the country's 10 largest cities, the "Pennsy", with some 10,000 route miles, by 1874, was the largest railroad company in the U.S.A. An ambitious railroad, the "Pennsy" eventually constructed one of the greatest stations ever built in the United States — New York Central — and was amongst the pioneers of electric traction. It possessed one of the largest electrified networks in the U.S.A., reflecting its important role as a carrier of commuters into major northeastern cities. The "Pennsy" became part of Penn Central in 1968 and Conrail in 1976.

FAR LEFT: Preserved as part of the Railroad Museum of Pennsylvania's collection at Strasburg, Pennsylvania, No. 7688 is a 2-8-0 of Class H10s built for the Pennsylvania Railroad by Lima in 1915. It was donated to the museum by the successor of the PRR, the Penn Central Corporation, in December 1979. *Derek Huntriss*

ABOVE: Now preserved, this 44-ton GE-built Bo-Bo switcher was originally Pennsylvania Railroad No. 9331. The locomotive is currently operational on the Strasburg Railroad in Pennsylvania. *Brian Solomon*

LEFT: Preserved Pennsylvania Railroad E8A No. 5711 makes a fine sight when recorded at Renova, Pennsylvania, in October 2003. *Brian Solomon*

Southern Pacific

One of the great names in U.S. railroading, the Southern Pacific first appeared in 1865. One of the subsidiary companies — Central Pacific (leased from 1885 and absorbed in 1955) — constructed the first transcontinental route in North America in conjunction with the Union Pacific, the great meeting being marked at Promontory Point, Utah, on May 10, 1869. The SP continued to grow rapidly, achieving a maximum route mileage of over 16,000 miles, including more than 1,000 miles of electrified line. Among records claimed by the SP was ownership of what was then the longest railroad bridge in the world — some 13 miles in length near Salt Lake City (now converted into an embankment) — and the longest combined road/rail bridge in the world, the Huey P. Long bridge at New Orleans. Notable companies taken over by the SP were the Denver & Rio Grande Western and the St Louis Southwestern railroads. In 1996 — almost a century after it was first mooted — SP merged with Union Pacific, with the new company retaining the UP name.

RIGHT: One of five fire-train locomotives operated by Southern Pacific. These engines were equipped with powerful pumps on top of the boiler, reels of hose, and other equipment in order to fight fires. During the summer, when there is a danger of fire in the sheds or along the track, these locomotives were kept in steam and manned with a full crew in order to be operational at a moment's notice. *Ian Allan Library*

OPPOSITE, ABOVE: A Southern Pacific locomotive, No. 3764, hauls a train of some 100 wagons without assistance up a gradient in the Sierra Nevada Mountains. *Southern Pacific*

OPPOSITE, BELOW: "Crossing Great Salt Lake on Southern Pacific" — a poster designed by Haines Hall promoting the streamlined services offered by Southern Pacific. The "Overland Limited" is pictured passing as the trains cross the Lake Tahoe line of the Southern Pacific. Heading towards the camera is Southern Pacific 4-6-2 No. 2461. *Southern Pacific*

FAR LEFT: The *City of Denver* was one of a number of streamline trains introduced by the Union Pacific in the 1930s. *Union Pacific*

LEFT: On July 6, 1955 Union Pacific No. 9000, the original 4-12-2, heads eastbound towards Omaha with freight. The locomotive was preserved after withdrawal. Introduced by Union Pacific in April 1926, a total of 88 locomotives of this wheel arrangement were delivered to the railroad between then and 1930 for use primarily on the company's line from Green River, Wyoming, to Council Bluffs, Iowa. These were the only locomotives with this wheel arrangement built for use in the U.S. *W. H. N. Rossiter*

BELOW LEFT: On May 19, 1981 a train of 75 grain hoppers heads westbound through Weben Canyon behind "SD40-2" No. 3686 and three "GP30s" Nos 806, 874, and 805. *P. J. Howard*

Union Pacific

Another legendary name in U.S. railroading history, Union Pacific's life began with the start of its section of the first transcontinental railway at a point near Omaha on June 10, 1865. Four years later, at Promontory Point, Utah, on May 10, 1869, the dream of constructing a through railway across the United States was achieved when the Union and Central Pacific lines met. Whilst the Central Pacific was destined for a relatively short independent existence, Union Pacific has gone from strength to strength to become one of the dominant forces in U.S. railroading. Already incorporating the Western Pacific, the Texas & Pacific, and the Missouri Pacific railroads, the UP expanded further in 1982 with the takeover of the Missouri-Kansas-Texas, and, in 1988, with the Chicago & North Western. In 1996 a further merger, this time with the Southern Pacific, saw the expanded Union Pacific emerge as one of the "Big Four" railroad companies, operating over more than 33,000 route miles.

"A railroad legacy spanning more than 140 years."
Union Pacific Historical Society

STATION TO STATION

"AMERICA'S GRANDEST RAILWAY TERMINAL"
~ PENNSYLVANIA RAILROAD ~
NEW PASSENGER STATION, BROAD STREET, PHILADELPHIA, U.S.A.

Although many early railways in Europe were designed specifically for freight traffic, the promoters soon realized that there was considerable additional revenue to be gained through the operation of passenger trains. In order to provide facilities for the passengers, the construction of stations or depots was necessary and, at the height of the railway age, most communities in the country would have had access to a station. However, facilities could vary dramatically from the simplest wayside halt with little more than a rudimentary platform and building, through to some of the grandest structures built in the years before World War 1. The finest examples in the United States were the Grand Central station in New York, built between 1911 and 1913, and the Washington Union station, built between 1903 and 1907.

ABOVE LEFT: The exterior of the old Pennsylvania station on the corner of 6th and B Streets in Washington D.C., as portrayed in the 1880s. *Library of Congress*

LEFT: Proudly proclaiming itself as "America's Grandest Railroad Station," Broad Street station, Philadelphia, is seen here in the early 1890s. *Library of Congress*

RIGHT: The railroads offered those who lived in the city the opportunity of traveling into the countryside for holidays and weekends. Here the station at Sylvan Beach, New York, is full of passengers awaiting their train back towards the city, c.1900. *Library of Congress*

ABOVE RIGHT: Hannover Junction station, Pennsylvania, photographed in 1863. *Library of Congress*

ABOVE: Independence station, Iowa, of the Chicago, Rock Island, & Pacific Railroad c.1909. *Library of Congress*

BELOW: In the early years of the 20th century the Pennsylvania Railroad announced its intention to extend its line into New York and to build a new station on the west side of Manhattan. This is a view of the finished station, taken from the northeast in c. 1911. The sheer size of the structure in comparison with its surroundings is striking. The station, amid much controversy, was to suffer demolition above platform level in the early 1960s when it was replaced by Madison Square Gardens. *Corbis HU043152*

Railroads in the 19th Century

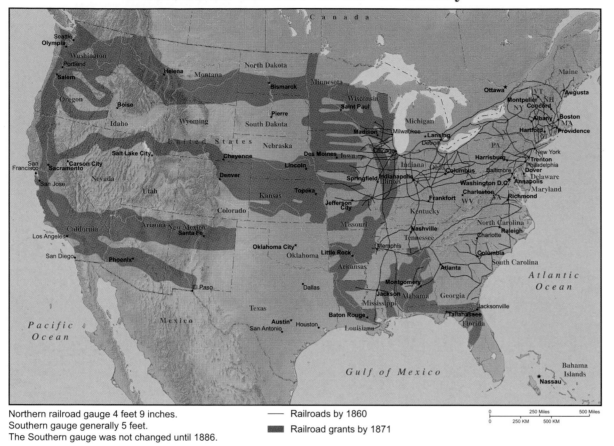

Northern railroad gauge 4 feet 9 inches.
Southern gauge generally 5 feet.
The Southern gauge was not changed until 1886.

— Railroads by 1860

▬ Railroad grants by 1871

By the Pacific Railway Acts, 1862-1864, railroad companies obtained the right of option to buy a wide belt of land on both sides of their route. Altogether 131 million acres were granted by Congress to the railroads, 39 million to the Northern Pacific. In 1935 President F.D. Roosevelt withdrew the unsold land for conservation and public use.

Class I Railroads in North America

United States, east of the Mississippi River

— CSX Transportation
— Norfolk Southern Railway

United States, west of the Mississippi River

— BNSF Railway
— Union Pacific Railroad
— Kansas City Southern Railway

Canada, with trackage extending into the United States

— Canadian National Railway
— Canadian Pacific Railway

Mexico, with no trackage in the United States

— Ferrocarril Mexicano
— Grupo Transportación Ferroviaria Mexicana (owned by the Kansas City Southern Railway)

Railroads in the Early 20th Century

— Railroads by 1913

50   **1965**   **1970**   **1975**   **1980**   **1985**   **1990**   **1995**   **2000**   **2005**   **2010**

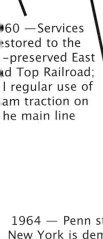

60 —Services restored to the -preserved East d Top Railroad; regular use of am traction on he main line

1970 — Amtrak established

Steamtown National Historic Site opened in Scranton, PA in 1995 having been established by Congress in 1986 to tell the story of steam railroading

2000 —The Acela high-speed titlting-train service between Boston and Washington opens

1980 —US railroads deregulated; Interstate Commerce Commission abolished

1964 — Penn station in New York is demolished; the outcry leads to the landmarks preservation act

1971 —opening of the preserved Cumbres & Toltec Scenic Railroad

1981 — D&RG Silverton Branch purchased for excursion service. The Durango and Silverton Narrow Gauge Railroad today runs 45 miles of scenic railways.

1976 —Failure of Penn Central; the last Railway Post Office (between New York and Washington) stops; Grand Central Terminal declared a National Historic Landmark

1973 —Work starts on the reconstruction of the Georgetown Loop Railroad

1967 —Final run of the New York Central's "20th Century Ltd"

PREVIOUS PAGE: The Cumbres and Toltec Scenic Railroad was originally laid down in 1880 and started carrying tourists in 1970. *Brian Solomon*

ABOVE: The two Shays of the Georgetown Loop Railroad make an impressive site as they cross the Devil's Gate High Bridge, which was reconstructed in the early 1980s. *Derek Huntriss*

RIGHT: New Dover, New Hampshire, station. *Brian Solomon*

BELOW RIGHT: The Baltimore & Ohio station at Laurel, Maryland. *Brian Solomon*

FAR RIGHT: The façade of Cincinnati Union station. *Brian Solomon*

WORKING THE RAILROADS

From the start the railroad industry was labor intensive. As already seen, construction of the railroads involved a vast number of manual workers and, once opened, the railroads offered myriad opportunities for employment. From those selling tickets in railroad stations, to those employed in maintenance and operation, the industry offered many job opportunities. Moreover, it was not just the direct employment offered by the railroads that helped the economy to grow in the late 19th century. Ancillary businesses — such as locomotive builders — also grew up, with companies such as Baldwin and Alco exporting their products worldwide.

ABOVE: Photographed in Corwith Yard, Chicago, in March 1943, a freight train of the Atchison, Topeka, & Santa Fe Railroad is blue flagged for inspection. The railroads relied heavily on manpower for the visual inspection of track and rolling stock in order to ensure smooth operation; some of these tasks have seen technology introduced that reduce the reliance upon the railroad staff. *Library of Congress*

ABOVE: In February 1943 a switchman is recorded at work on the Indiana Harbor Belt Line railroad yard. Although switches were generally controlled from cabins when intensively used, in yards and less well-used lines, switches were and are still generally thrown manually. *Library of Congress*

FAR LEFT: The onboard crew represented the public face of the railroad industry to the passengers. Here a porter is pictured passing over a glass of water to a passenger in a sleeping car during the first decade of the 20th century. *Library of Congress*

LEFT: A towerman, R. W. Mayberry, sits in the tower at Proviso Yard, in Chicago, in March 1943. The huge freight marshalling yards required efficient work from the towers to ensure that the contents of each individual train were effectively combined. *Library of Congress*

BELOW: In an era before the use of air became practical, and when the bulk of communication was via physical rather than electronic means, the railroads provided an essential link in the movement and sorting of mail. This is the interior of a mail train in the early years of the 20th century. *Library of Congress*

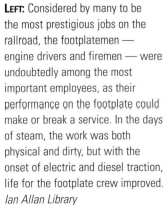

LEFT: Considered by many to be the most prestigious jobs on the railroad, the footplatemen — engine drivers and firemen — were undoubtedly among the most important employees, as their performance on the footplate could make or break a service. In the days of steam, the work was both physical and dirty, but with the onset of electric and diesel traction, life for the footplate crew improved. *Ian Allan Library*

ABOVE: Once laid, the track required regular maintenance. Here, in April 1943, a section crew is at work on the line of the Chicago, Milwaukee, St Paul, & Pacific Railroad at Bensenville, Illinois. *Library of Congress*

ABOVE: All locomotives and rolling stock required regular maintenance: this locomotive of the Chicago & North Western Railroad is under repair in the railroad's 40th Street shed in December 1942. *Library of Congress*

THE GREAT STEAM LOCOMOTIVES

The "American" 4-4-0

In February 1836 Henry H. Campbell, the Chief Engineer of the Philadelphia, Germantown, & Norris Railway, received a patent for the design of the 4-4-0 locomotive and work on its construction began immediately. Campbell's locomotive, however, had one serious drawback — a tendency to derail as all four axles were set within a rigid frame. The following year, Eastwick & Harrison constructed a 4-4-0, named Hercules, for the Beaver Meadow Railroad; this was the first to include a leading truck, which improved the suitability of the type for the tight curves and varying grades of the early railroads. The original design of the 4-4-0 type owed much to the pioneering work of the English engineer Edward Bury, whose use of bar frames and four-coupled driving wheels linked by coupling rods ensured maximum power but relatively light axle loads on sharply curved track. This was important for the early railway lines constructed in the U.S.A. and Bury's influence on U.S.

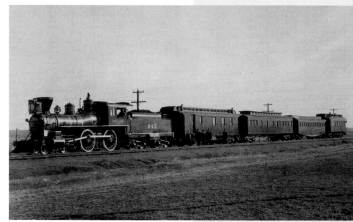

locomotive development was assured once his company, Bury, Curtis, & Kennedy, started to export locomotives to the U.S. market. The name "American" was first attached to the type in 1872 by the *Railroad Gazette*; prior to that date the locomotives were known either as the "Standard" or "Eight-wheeler" type.

The 4-4-0 was perhaps the epitome of the steam locomotive during the early years of railroad operation in the U.S.A. A total of 20,000 were built between 1840 and 1890 and, in 1870, some 85 percent of all U.S. steam locomotives were of this wheel arrangement; in all, some 25,000 4-4-0s were built for use on U.S. railroads. However, as the weight of trains grew, so the need for more powerful designs resulted, and the 4-4-0 was gradually superseded. By 1900, construction of the 4-4-0 had largely ceased, although the type continued to be favored on branch lines. Baldwin built the last of the type in 1945 by for the United Railways of Yucatan.

TOP: This 4-4-0 — *North Star* of the Central Vermont Railroad — was delivered in the early 1860s. *Canadian National Railways*

ABOVE: 4-4-0 No. 173 was the first locomotive to be built completely at the Central Pacific Railroad's workshops at Sacramento, in 1872. *Union Pacific*

RIGHT: Built at the Globe Loco Works, Boston, Mass, in 1849, *Pioneer* was brought to California in 1855 — the first locomotive in the state — by ship sailing via Cape Horn. It operated over the Sacramento Valley Railroad until withdrawal in 1888 when it was scrapped. It was the only inside-cylinder locomotive ever to operate on the Pacific coast. *Ian Allan Library*

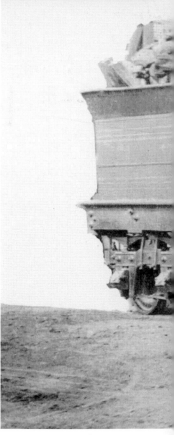

"O the engineer's joys! to go with a locomotive!
To hear the hiss of steam, the merry shriek, the
steam-whistle, the laughing locomotive!
To push with resistless way and speed
off in the distance."

Walt Whitman, *A Song of Joys*

The "Atlantic" 4-4-2

The first "Atlantic"-type 4-4-2 locomotives were built for the Lehigh Valley Railroad by the Vulcan Iron Works of Wilkes-Barre, Pennsylvania, in 1888. The nickname was acquired as a result of an order placed in 1894 by the Atlantic Coast Line. The locomotives, of which some 1,900 were constructed, were primarily built for use on express passenger trains, where their large driving wheels — often of more than six feet in diameter — were ideal for obtaining high speeds. However, the type was less well suited for routes with heavy gradients, where slower speeds were the norm, and on long distance runs.

FAR LEFT: Chicago, Cleveland, Cincinnati & St Louis Railroad No. 394. *Ian Allan Library*

ABOVE: On display at the Pennsylvania Railroad Museum, Strasburg, Pennsylvania, is ex-Pennsylvania Railroad 4-4-2 No. 7002. This locomotive, originally number 8063, was built at the railroad's workshops at Juniata in 1902 as one of the railroad's "E7s" class of "Atlantic" locomotives. The locomotive, which is in the guise of the locomotive that held the speed record of 127.1 mph in 1905, was donated to the museum by Penn Central in December 1979. It last operated in January 1989. *Derek Huntriss*

LEFT: The "Atlantic" type— exemplified by No. 1444 of the Atchison, Topeka & Santa Fe Railroad—was designed primarily for fast passenger services. *Ian Allan Library*

"[Atlantics on the Philadelphia & Reading Railroad] — the fastest railway run in the world in the first decade of the [20th] century."

Cecil J. Allen

The "Mogul" 2-6-0

While the first locomotives of this wheel arrangement were produced as early as 1852, it was not until 1858 that Levi Bissell patented the single-axle swiveling truck required. Built in the 1850s, the early examples of the 2-6-0 had the leading axle rigidly mounted on the frame and can be regarded more as 0-8-0s with leading set of wheels unpowered. The leading axle was, therefore, merely a means of allowing better weight distribution. The first true 2-6-0 with a swiveling truck was built for the Louisville & Nashville Railroad in 1860. While the 2-6-0s offered increased pulling power, there was also an increased tendency to derail over the earlier 4-4-0 design. Many contemporary engineers attributed this fault to a lack of weight on the leading truck, and in 1864, William S. Hudson patented a truck with equalized suspension. In all, some 11,000 "Moguls" were constructed for use on railroads in North America.

RIGHT: Among the locomotives on static display at the Railroad Museum of Pennsylvania at Strasburg is Virginia & Truckee No. 20. Named Tahoe, this locomotive was originally constructed by Baldwin in 1875 and is one of two 2-6-0 type locomotives owned by the V&TR that survive in preservation. A second example, No. 13, is on display at the California State Railroad Museum. *Brian Solomon*

ABOVE: A second example of the Canadian National Railway's (CNR) Class E-10a is also operational in the U.S.A. No. 91 is based at the Middletown & Hummelstown Railroad located at Middletown Pennsylvania. The locomotive was originally built in 1910 and was restored to an operational condition in 2003. It is pictured here in September 2007. *Brian Solomon*

LEFT: Wilmington & Western 2-6-0 No. 92 photographed during a run from Greenbank to Mount Cuba, Delaware. *H. Bongaardt*

LEFT: Pictured near Stillwater, Minnesota, in August 1996, Northern Pacific No. 328 was secured for restoration in 1976 but it was not until 1981 that work was completed. The locomotive was built by Alco at their works at Patterson, New Jersey, as one of a batch of ten Class S-10 4-6-0s that were originally ordered by the Chicago Southern Railroad but were ultimately delivered in 1907 to Northern Pacific. No. 328 was one of the last two survivors, being withdrawn in March 1950. Originally scheduled for scrapping, the locomotive was secured for static display by the Minnesota Railfan's Association and donated to Stillwater. *Brian Solomon*

RIGHT: One of eight steam locomotives previously owned by the Chicago & North Western Railroad to survive, No. 1385 is now based at the Mid-Continent Railway Museum of North Freedom, Wisconsin, and is the only example of the railroad's steam locomotive roster to be operational, although it is currently undergoing restoration. Built by Alco at its Schenectady Works in March 1907, it was one of 325 members of the railroad's Class R-1 — the single largest type of locomotive owned by the C&NW — and is now the sole survivor of the type. No. 1385 was withdrawn in 1956 and was secured for preservation by the Mid-Continent Railway Museum seven years later. It is seen here on 8 October 1994 disguised as DL&WR No. 1053. *Brian Solomon*

RIGHT: A "Ten-Wheeler" No. 155 delivered to the Chicago & East Illinois Railroad. *Ian Allan Library*

The "Ten-Wheeler" 4-6-0

Named *Chesapeake*, the first 4-6-0 was delivered by Norris in March 1847 to the Philadelphia & Reading Railroad. This was followed by two other early examples, New Hampshire for the Boston & Maine, and *Susquehanna* for the Erie. The number of 4-6-0s constructed grew rapidly from the 1860s onwards as railroads began to purchase locomotives for specific purposes rather than the traditional "maid of all work", the 4-4-0. Locomotives of this arrangement continued to be delivered through to the early 20th century, although increasingly they were superseded by larger and more powerful designs. In all, some 15,500 "Ten-wheelers" operated on North American railroads.

The "Pacific" 4-6-2

The first 4-6-2 — or "Pacific" — locomotive in the world was constructed at the Vulcan Iron Works, Wilkes-Barre, Pennsylvania in 1886 for use on the Lehigh Valley Railroad. Baldwin constructed the first "standard" 4-6-2, as opposed to the foreshortened design built for the LVR, in 1901 for export to New Zealand. Some 6,000 were constructed for use in the U.S.A., as the wheel arrangement allowed for use on express passenger services and the enlarged boiler allowed for great tractive effort than the earlier "Atlantic" design, with the result that most railroad operators ran some "Pacific" designs.

ABOVE: Pacific No. 623, of the Chicago & Alton Railroad. *Ian Allan Library*

RIGHT: Baltimore & Ohio Pacific No. 5329 *President Cleveland* photographed when newly delivered from the railroad's own workshops at Mount Clare. This type of locomotive was designed for fast through passenger services. *B&OR*

FAR RIGHT: Some 6,000 4-6-2s were constructed for use on U.S. railroads; the single largest operator of the type was the Pennsylvania Railroad, which owned 697 of the type including 425 Class K4s (the single largest class of steam locomotive constructed for use in the U.S.) — such as No. 1737 illustrated here, which was the first of the class to enter service having been built at the railroad's own workshops at Altoona in 1914. *Pennsylvania Railroad*

"I asked Pat[rick E. Crowley, NYC President All Lines] if we should name the engine and if he cared about that at all … Finally he spoke, 'Let's call her the Hudson after the Hudson River.' I agreed immediately … It was a natural."

Paul Kiefer **1961**

BELOW: Another significant user of the "Hudson" locomotive was the Atchison, Topeka, & Santa Fe, which operated 16 of the type. The first ten, built by Baldwin, were delivered in 1927, with the remaining six, again built by Baldwin, following a decade later. In December 1937 one of the type, No. 3461, operated a service all the way from Los Angeles to Chicago, the distance of some 2,227 miles representing the longest distance ever operated in a single trip by a steam engine. No. 3450, the first of the original ten, is illustrated here; this is one of two of the type to survive in preservation, being displayed at the LA County Fairplex, Pomona, California. *Ian Allan Library*

The "Hudson" 4-6-4

The 4-6-4 locomotive was originally developed by American Locomotive Works at Schenectady, New York, for use on the New York Central Railroad and was named after the river that ran parallel to the railroad as it headed into the country. A total of 487 4-6-4s were constructed for use on railroads in North America; of these, 407 saw service with 17 different railroad companies. Almost half of the total, 195, were operated by the New York Central with other major users being the Michigan Central, with 30, and the Cleveland, Cincinnati, Chicago, & St Louis Railroad, also with 30.

LEFT: In 1927, to mark the centenary of the meeting that inaugurated the Baltimore and Ohio, a centenary exhibition and pageant was held. Apart from examples of locomotives and rolling stock from the B&O, examples from other railroads also operated. Here a New York Central "Hudson" 4-6-4 No. 5205 passes the grandstand; a long line of further exhibits can be seen in the background. *Ian Allan Library*

The "Consolidation" 2-8-0

The first 2-8-0 was built by Baldwin in 1866 and was named *Consolidation* to mark the union of the Lehigh Valley and Lehigh & Mahoney railroads. Growth in the use of 2-8-0s was relatively slow after their initial introduction, and it was not until 1875, when the Pennsylvania Railroad selected the type as its primary locomotive for freight traffic, that orders grew. In service, the railroads discovered that the locomotives were able to haul up to twice as much as the earlier 4-4-0s for considerably less cost. The type was later to become the most common steam locomotive on U.S. railroads.

ABOVE RIGHT: "Consolidation," No. 835 of the Grand Trunk Pacific Railroad. *Ian Allan Library*

RIGHT: Southern Pacific 2-8-0 No. 3420 pictured at El Paso, Texas, in September 1962. *Harry Luff Collection/Online Transport Archive*

FAR RIGHT: Currently operational on the Western Maryland Scenic Railroad (WMSR), No. 734 is a 2-8-0 built by Baldwin in 1916 for the Lake Superior & Ishpeming Railroad. Originally preserved in the Illinois Railroad Museum, it was acquired by the WMSR in 1991 and restored to operational condition in the following year. It is pictured here in 2000. *Derek Huntriss*

The "Mikado" 2-8-2

The first 2-8-2 was constructed in 1884 for the Chicago & Calumet Terminal Railroad, although the previous year the Lehigh Valley Railroad had converted one of its 2-10-0s into a 2-8-2 in order to reduce the wear on the last set of driving wheels. The type acquired it nickname "Mikado" in 1893 following the delivery by Baldwin of a batch of narrow-gauge locomotives to a railroad operator in Japan. The delivery was contemporaneous with the opening of the Gilbert and Sullivan opera *The Mikado* and

the name stuck. Following the Japanese attack on Pearl Harbor in December 1941 an alternative, less Japanese name, the "MacArthur" (after General Douglas MacArthur), was adopted, although postwar the traditional name was again widely adopted. Designed primarily for freight traffic, the 2-8-2 was widely used on U.S. railroads, with 14,000 constructed in the country and some 9,500 actually used on U.S. railroads.

ABOVE: The "K-36" 2-8-2s were the last 10 narrow gauge locomotives constructed for use on the Denver & Rio Grande Western. Built by Baldwin at Philadelphia in 1925, no fewer than nine of the type survive in preservation on the Durango & Silverton and Cumbres & Toltec railroads. The one casualty — No. 485 — fell into a turntable pit at Salida, California, in 1955 and was subsequent cannibalized for parts. This view records one of those preserved on the Durango & Silverton Railroad — No. 481. *Brian Solomon*

LEFT: Duluth & North Minnesota Railroad No. 14, which is currently stored operational at the Lake Superior Transportation Museum, Duluth, Minnesota, is the only surviving steam locomotive from the D&NMR. The locomotive was constructed by Baldwin in 1913 primarily for use on the region's logging trains. When this work ceased, the locomotive was sold to the Lake Superior & Ishpeming Railroad, where it was to survive until 1959, before being sold to the Inland Stone Division of Gulliver, Michigan. Following preservation, the locomotive was restored to operational condition in 1992. It is pictured here in July 1996. *Brian Solomon*

LEFT: The East Broad Top Railroad is now the last narrow gauge railroad east of the Rocks, but its survival was by no means certain as, in 1956 when the original line closed, the track and equipment were acquired by the Kovalchick Salvage Co. of Indiana, Pennsylvania. Passenger services were initially restored in 1960 to mark the centenary of the towns of Orbisonia and Rockhill. Such was the success of this operation that the service was maintained and, in 1964, the line was designated a National Historic Landmark. The line owns a number of steam locomotives, including six "Mikado" type locomotives. Built in 1918 by Baldwin, East Broad Top No. 17 was the second largest "Mikado" to operate on the line. Initially restored for service for the line's reopening in 1960, the locomotive, pictured here in October 1997, has been out of service since October 2001 and is at present stored in the railroad's roundhouse.. *Brian Solomon*

The "Berkshire" 2-8-4

Developed by the Lima Locomotive Works of Lima, Ohio, the first 2-8-4 "Berkshire" locomotives were built for the Boston & Albany Railroad for use on its line in the Berkshire Mountains — hence the nickname between 1926 and 1930 following on from a prototype constructed in 1924. The trailing bogie in the earlier 2-8-2 design had proved inadequate as it could support only a limited weight from the locomotive's firebox and cab; the additional trailing axle therefore allowed for a greater size of firebox and thus a more powerful locomotive. Often regarded as the epitome of steam "super power," examples of the type were supplied to a number of railroads by Lima, Alco, and Baldwin. Between 1924 and 1949 more than 600 locomotives of this type were delivered to U.S. railroads.

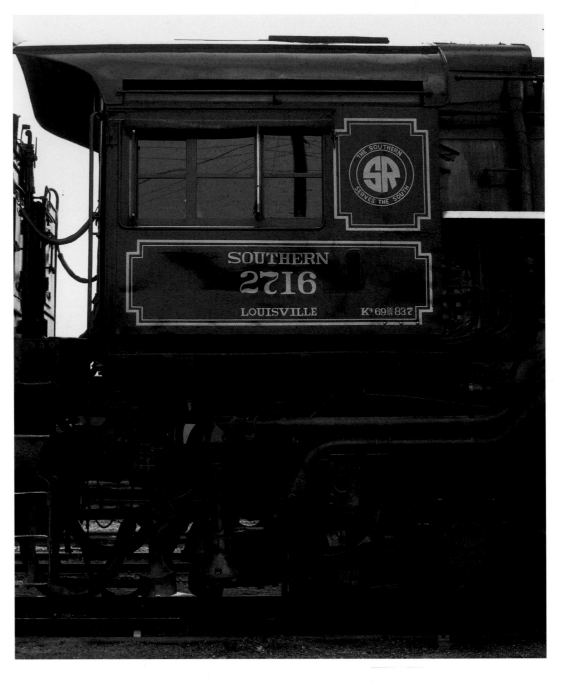

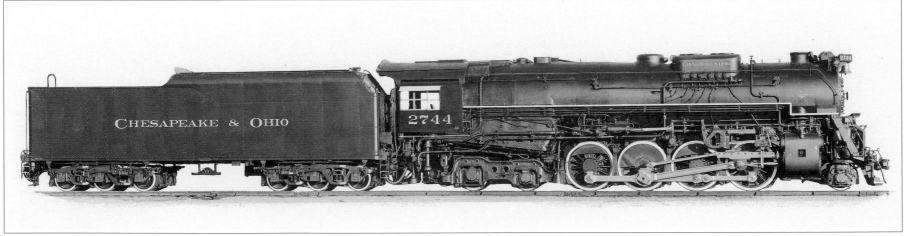

LEFT: A close-up of the cab of ex-Chesapeake & Ohio Class K-4 2-8-4 No. 2716 in the guise of Southern Railway No. 2716. The locomotive was originally one of 90 2-8-4s delivered to the railroad by Alco and Lima between 1943 and 1947. For a period in the early 1980s the locomotive, in the guise of Southern 2716, was operated as part of the railroad's excursion fleet, but is now restored to original C&O livery, and is on static display at the Kentucky Railway Museum, New Haven, Kentucky. A total of 12 examples of the type survive. *Derek Huntriss*

BELOW LEFT: The Chesapeake & Ohio were major users of 2-8-4 type as exemplified by No. 2744; sister locomotive No. 2716 is also preserved. *Ian Allan Library*

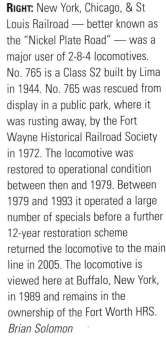

RIGHT: New York, Chicago, & St Louis Railroad — better known as the "Nickel Plate Road" — was a major user of 2-8-4 locomotives. No. 765 is a Class S2 built by Lima in 1944. No. 765 was rescued from display in a public park, where it was rusting away, by the Fort Wayne Historical Railroad Society in 1972. The locomotive was restored to operational condition between then and 1979. Between 1979 and 1993 it operated a large number of specials before a further 12-year restoration scheme returned the locomotive to the main line in 2005. The locomotive is viewed here at Buffalo, New York, in 1989 and remains in the ownership of the Fort Worth HRS. *Brian Solomon*

LEFT: Southern Pacific "Mountain" type 4-8-2 No. 4367. This was built at the railroad's own workshops at Sacramento in 1929. With 6 ft 1 in. driving wheels and a tractive effort of 67,660 lb, the locomotives were designed for hauling express passenger services over the grades of the railroad's mountain route from Los Angeles to El Paso, Texas. This route was some 875 miles in length and went from 30 ft above sea level to over 5,000 ft at one point, while also traversing the Imperial Valley, where the railroad's trackbed was 230 ft below sea level. The locomotive was designed to travel at 60 mph on the level and 20 mph on the grades of up to 105 ft per mile. *Ian Allan Library*

ABOVE: New York Central 4-8-2 No. 3135. *Ian Allan Library*

BELOW: A 4-8-2 "Mountain" of the Atchison, Topeka, & Santa Fe Railroad, No. 3448, heads the "California Limited" near Morris, Kansas. *Ian Allan Library*

The "Mountain" 4-8-2

Developed originally in New Zealand, where the first example was built in 1908, the "Mountain" 4-8-2 first saw service in the U.S.A. with the Chesapeake & Ohio. By the first decade of the 20th century, the C&O required more powerful locomotives in order to haul its services over the Allegheny Mountains as trains grew in size. Between 1911 and 1948, a total of 2,128 locomotives with this wheel arrangement were delivered to 39 different railroads in the U.S.A. Of these, the two largest operators of the type were the Pennsylvania, with 301 examples, and the New York Central, with 600 (known as "Mohawks"), railroads.

LEFT: Chesapeake & Ohio Class J3a 4-8-4 No. 614 is now owned in an operational condition by Iron Horse Enterprises Inc. of Sackets Harbor, New York. The locomotive was constructed by Lima in June 1948 and was the last mainline steam locomotive to be constructed for use on an American railroad. Designed for use on the railroad's express passenger services — such as the "George Washington" — between Richmond, Virginia, and Chicago, the locomotive was successful, but destined to have a short life. Withdrawal came in 1952 with the rapid elimination of steam traction on U.S. railroads. Following withdrawal, the locomotive languished on a siding in Kentucky until cosmetic restoration was undertaken in 1976. *Brian Solomon*

BELOW LEFT: Ohio Central 4-8-4 No. 6325 photographed with a special on the old Pennsylvania Railroad Panhandle line on October 19, 2002. *Brian Solomon*

BELOW: Union Pacific Class FEF-3 No. 844 was the last of 45 4-8-4 locomotives delivered to the railroad between 1937 and 1944 and was, in fact, the last new steam locomotive to be acquired by the railroad. On withdrawal in 1960, the locomotive was preserved by the railroad and is now used on special services. For a period, No. 844 carried the number 8444 in order to distinguish it from a diesel in the 8xx series. On the withdrawal of the diesel in June 1989, No. 844 reverted to its original number. It is seen here operating a special between Stirling and Denver. *Derek Huntriss*

The "Northern" 4-8-4

The 4-8-4 was a logical development of the earlier 4-8-2 and 4-6-4 designs. It allowed for a combination of the 4-8-2's increased tractive effort, as a result of more weight on the driving wheels, with the 4-6-4's enlarged firebox. The first 4-8-4 was delivered in January 1927 by ALCO for Northern Pacific. The extra large firebox that the 4-8-4 allowed was necessary to accommodate the low grade of bituminous coal that the NPR used. Known as the "Northern" type on NPR, other railroads gave the type alternative names. Thus, they became known, for example, as "Potomacs" on the Western Maryland Railroad and "Niagaras" on the New York Central. Operated by 32 U.S. railroads, the type was well suited for fast passenger and express freight services, and 937 were built for operation.

Articulated locomotives

The French locomotive designer Anatole Mallet was responsible for the development of the first compound articulated locomotives during the 1880s. The strength of the design was that it allowed for maximum power with light axle loadings, the latter being essential on lines constructed lightly and with sharp curves. The first Mallet compound locomotive in the United States was delivered to the B&O in 1903 and this was to set a pattern for future steam locomotive design in the U.S.A., culminating in designs such as the 2-8-8-4 used by lines such as the Northern Pacific, and the "Big Boys" of Union Pacific. The vast majority of the articulated locomotives used on

U.S. railroads, however, used simple rather than compound expansion (and were not true Mallet-type locomotives other than in their use of his principle of articulation). Constructed by Alco between 1941 and 1944, the 25 members of the UP's class of 4-8-8-4 "Big Boy" locomotives were regarded as the most powerful steam locomotives ever built and were produced to help meet the need for ever more powerful locomotives to cope with the wartime freight traffic.

ABOVE: A total of 25 "Big Boy" 4-8-8-4 locomotives were built for the Union Pacific in two batches: numbers 4000-19 were constructed in 1941, and the final five, numbers 4020-24, followed in 1944. The last of the type were withdrawn from service in late 1962. A total of eight members of this impressive class of locomotive remain extant, although none is currently operational. Union Pacific No. 4017 is displayed at the National Railroad Museum, Green Bay, Wisconsin. *Brian Solomon*

ABOVE RIGHT: Northern Pacific Class Z-6 4-6-6-4 No. 5106 recorded with freight at Butts, Montana, in the Rocky Mountains. *Northern Pacific Railway*

LEFT: In 1909 the first of 2-8-8-2 was built by Baldwin for use on the Southern Pacific Railroad. A subsequent order was for the first of the railroad's cab-forward locomotives, which were designed to deal with the long tunnels and snow-sheds of its line through the Sierra Nevada Mountains. In the confined space of tunnels, exhaust fumes from the locomotives blew back into the cab and could cause near asphyxiation among the locomotive crews; by placing the cab at the front of the locomotive, this problem was avoided. Here one of the cab-forward locomotives is recorded approaching Glendale, California, with a service from San Francisco. *Ian Allan Library*

RIGHT: Pictured in service on the restored Georgetown Loop Railroad in Colorado is Shay No.14, originally built in 1916 for operation on lumber lines in California. Following the end of its industrial career, it was operational on the Georgetown Loop Railroad between 1980 and 2004, when it was transferred in an operational condition for storage at the Colorado Railroad Museum It is seen here on October 3, 1993.
Derek Huntriss

TOURIST RAILWAYS

Almost from the dawn of the railway age, promoters realized that there was considerable commercial potential in the construction of lines specifically for tourists to be able to gain access to popular sites. In 1869 the Mount Washington cog railway opened; other examples of tourist-oriented routes included the Grand Canyon Railroad of the Santa Fe, and the Georgetown Loop. However, just as the major railroads suffered from the rise of the internal combustion engine, so too did many of these pioneering tourist railways and, with exceptions (such as the Mount Washington line), the majority closed. This was not necessarily the end, however, as a number of these lines (including both the Grand Canyon and Georgetown Loop lines) have been resurrected partly as a means of reducing road traffic.

LEFT: A single unit ascends the Manitou & Pikes Peak Railway; the view shows the center, cogged, track that allows locomotives and rolling stock to ascend and descend steep grades safely. *Harry Luff/Online Transport Archive*

BELOW: Mount Washington No. 6 pictured at the summit in July 1971; the view shows to good effect the arrangement of the inclined boiler essential if a steam locomotive is to operate safely over gradients encountered on lines such as the Mount Washington. *Harry Luff Collection/Online Transport Archive*

TRAVELING IN STYLE

When the first railroads were opened in Britain there was concern that traveling at the relatively high speeds of which even the primitive railroads were capable would be beyond the capacity of the human frame to survive. In the event, however, such fears proved ill-founded but the accommodation provided by the early passenger trains was undoubtedly Spartan. Often derived from contemporary stagecoach designs, these early carriages offered little protection to the travelers, but it was not long before improved passenger cars started to offer levels of comfort unavailable elsewhere. As transcontinental routes were constructed, so journey time became longer and the need to provide sleeping and restaurant cars became greater. It was the poor quality of existing facilities that encouraged George Pullman to establish his eponymous business in the 1860s, and by the first decades of the 20th century the railroads were competing to provide ever more luxurious accommodation for passenger. Observation cars, for example, allowed passengers on long transcontinental journeys to appreciate better the grandeur of the landscape, but, within a generation, the rise of the private automobile and internal air travel meant that such luxury was to become outdated.

ABOVE RIGHT: Passenger accommodation on the early B&O was relatively primitive and owed much to the contemporary stagecoach — as this reconstruction shows. *Ian Allan Library*

RIGHT: A double-deck train belonging to the Long Island Railroad. Each car could accommodate 132 passengers as opposed to only 72 in conventional cars. *National Archives*

FAR RIGHT: Happy departures: a series of special trains was run in November 1955 in order to transport the crews of 33 U.S. Navy ships being transferred from East Coast to West Coast bases. *National Archives*

ABOVE: Described as a "modern interior" at the time, this was the scene inside a New York Central coach in 1946. *Brian Solomon*

RIGHT: "K-36" No. 484, based on the Cumbres & Toltec Scenic Railroad, recorded at Antonito, Colorado. *New York Central System*

BELOW: A view from the Strasburg Railroad. *Derek Huntriss*

LEFT: The opulence of early 20th century rolling stock is shown to good effect in this view of the interior of the *Martha Washington* dining car. *Ian Allan Library*

RIGHT A sleeper compartment on board a Union Pacific train on the Los Angeles-New York run in December 1934. *National Archives*

FAR RIGHT The dining car of the "20th Century Limited" of the New York Central Railroad. This was one of 16 cars that formed the train. The service, which operated from 1902 until 1967, was one of the most famous passenger trains in the world and, in its heyday, was noted as being amongst the most luxurious to operate. The concept of red carpet treatment arose as a result of passengers walking to and from the train at either New York or Chicago over a specially designed crimson carpet. *National Archives*

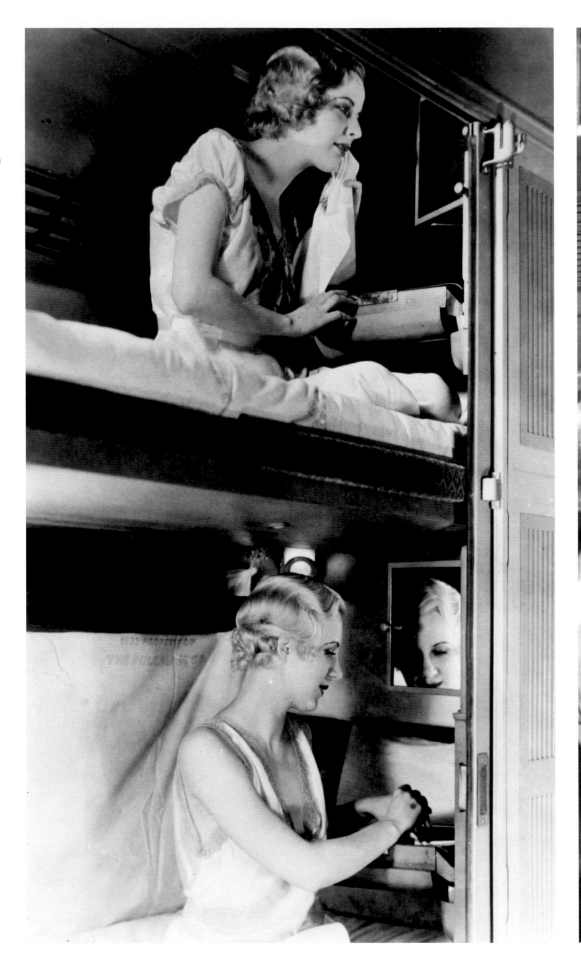

THE RAILWAYS AND WORLD WAR

Although the Civil War had had a dramatic and destructive impact on the United States' nascent railroad industry, the effect of the two world wars was equally important. One of the first actions after the declaration of war in 1917 was the placing of the railroad industry under federal control on December 28, 1917. This allowed the government to work the network as a single entity, to eliminate wasteful competition, and to allocate resources where they were needed. With William G. McAdoo as director-general, state control lasted for 26 months. However, the railroad companies were not satisfied either by the rental paid by the government for the use of the track and equipment, nor by the level of maintenance undertaken during this period. The railroad companies determined that, in the event of a future conflict, such state control should not be permitted again, and, during World War II, they achieved this. On December 18, 1941 President Roosevelt created the Office of Defense Transportation under Joseph Eastman to ensure co-ordination, but the railroads themselves maintained their own independence.

ABOVE: One of the revolutions that occurred as a result of the two world wars was the employment of women in jobs that had been traditionally been undertaken by men. Here two women are cleaning a Chicago & North Western Railroad "H" class locomotive in April 1943. *Library of Congress*

LEFT: Following the Japanese attack on Pearl Harbor in December 1941, the authorities moved quickly to intern all those of Japanese origin. Trains were used to evacuate the large numbers involved to the assembly centers. Here, in early 1942, evacuees await departure from Los Angeles station to Santa Anita Assembly Center. *Library of Congress*

BELOW: "A Speedy Termination of the War" — a wartime poster designed by Ernest Hamlin Baker exhorts railroad workers to do their part to help defeat the Germans and Japanese in World War II. *Swim Ink2, LLC/Corbis AAED002410*

A SPEEDY TERMINATION OF THE WAR

This depends more than anything else on the support the United States gives the Allies. Our country cannot do justice to the job, unless railroad men get busy and do their part.... Are you awake to your responsibility?

THE NATION IS COUNTING ON YOU

Apart from the structural changes required, there were also social changes wrought as a result of war. With vast numbers of men required to serve in the forces, women were recruited in large numbers to fulfill tasks such as locomotive cleaning that had traditionally been a male preserve. Moreover, there was a vast increase in the production of munitions and military equipment, with many workshops diverted from peacetime work to the construction of aircraft or tanks. The railway workshops were no exception, although the need for railroad equipment to assist the military resulted in large numbers of new locomotives being constructed in both world wars for shipment overseas. One notable design to emerge during World War II was the classic 2-8-0, the "S160" class of locomotive built between 1942 and 1946 on behalf of the United States Army Transportation Corps to the design of Major J. W. Marsh. Built by Lima, Alco, and Baldwin, a total of 2,120 locomotives were constructed, with many of the type initially seeing service in Britain before being shipped to the continent.

THE STREAMLINED ERA

While the 1930s represented a decade of struggle for the railroad industry, they were also years when the industry produced some of the most stylish locomotive designs and services. It was the era of streamlining, first launched by the Union Pacific's City of Salina in 1934. Diesel-powered locomotives, first introduced in the late 1920s, were both cleaner and offered great potential for stylish design, but it was not only the diesel locomotive that achieved streamlining during the 1930s. The passenger steam locomotive was also restyled. The first streamlined steam locomotive was the Commodore Vanderbilt of the New York Central in 1934. One of the most influential designers of this period was a French émigré, Raymond Loewy (1893–1986), who fostered a close relationship with the Pennsylvania Railroad, designing both steam and electric locomotives for the company.

RIGHT: In 1937 the Santa Fe launched its diesel-powered "Super Chief" service. Only 130 minutes were permitted for the 202 miles between La Junta and Dodge City, and, with an average speed of 87.2 mph, this was then the fastest railway service in the world. *Ian Allan Library*

BELOW: In 1934 the CB&QR launched the "Burlington Zephyr" — a diesel-powered three-coach articulated set that provided seating accommodation for 72 passengers as well as space for baggage and post. This is the brochure produced by the railway to launch the service. *Ian Allan Library*

LEFT: A postcard produced around 1941 for the Florida Sunbeam, which connected New York with the Sunshine State. Running southward, the train first traversed the New York Central, switched to Southern Railway trackage, and then finished its journey on the Seaboard Air Line. *Lake Country Museum/Corbis LW001270*

RIGHT: Built in January 1942 at the railroad's Roanoke Workshops, Norfolk & Western Class J 4-8-4 No. 604 heads westbound from Roanoke station with a service from Norfolk, Virginia, to Cincinnati, Ohio, a distance of 676.5 miles. *Ian Allan Library*

BELOW: A line-up of Santa Fe streamlined trains at Chicago. These are, from the left: the "Super Chief," an all-standard sleeping car train; "El Capitan," the all-coach train; the "Chief," a daily standard sleeping car train; a second "Super Chief"; and a second "El Capitan". The "Super Chief" and "El Capitan" operated twice weekly between Chicago and Los Angeles on a 40-hour schedule in each direction, and the "Chief" operated between the same points on a 48-hour schedule. *Santa Fe Railway*

RIGHT: B&OR Pacific No. 6502 was constructed for use on the Cincinnatian luxury train from Baltimore to Cincinnati, which was launched in January 1947. *B&O*

LEFT: Preserved as a static exhibit at Steamtown is ex-Canadian Pacific 4-4-4 No 2929, which was built originally in 1938. *Harry Luff Collection/© Online Transport Archive*

BELOW: One of the most stylish and colorful of all preserved American steam locomotives is undoubtedly Southern Pacific's streamlined 4-8-4, No. 4449, which is currently based at the Brooklyn Roundhouse, in Portland, Oregon, from where it operates a handful of special services each year. The locomotive was built by Lima and delivered to the railroad in May 1941. The red, black, and orange "Daylight" livery reflects the passenger trains of the same name that the locomotive was designed to haul. No. 4449 was withdrawn in 1957 and initially placed on static display in Portland, Oregon. In 1974 it was rescued and restored for use during the 1976 Bicentenary celebrations. *Brian Solomon*

DIESEL TRACTION

The invention of the diesel engine by the German Rudolf Diesel at the end of the 19th century was ultimately to spell the end of steam. Using oil, rather than gasoline, the diesel engine was cheaper to fuel, but the early designs were too cumbersome to be used in locomotives and it was not until the 1920s that the first practical diesel-electric — where the diesel engine powers a generator that in turn creates electricity to drive the train — locomotive was built. The major breakthrough came as a result of research by General Motors, led by Charles Kettering, which used lightweight alloys to improve yet further the power/weight ratio. A major factor in the growth of diesel traction was the creation of the Electro-Motive Division (EMD) of General Motors in 1935, which would ultimately become the largest manufacturer of diesel locomotives in the world. In 1936, with the opening of a new factory at La Grange, Illinois, production of standardized locomotives commenced. EMD-built locomotives were to become the face of U.S. railroads — even competitors adopted designs similar to those emerging from La Grange. Other U.S. manufacturers, such as ALCO, followed GM in the construction of diesel-powered locomotives and a vast number of diesel designs soon began to emerge.

Above: A 900 hp diesel locomotive supplied to the New York Central Railroad in 1928 for use on passenger trains. *Ian Allan Library*

Above right: The first General Motors "FT" locomotives emerged from the new La Grange factory in 1938. Among customers for this widely used type was Union Pacific. *Union Pacific*

Right: Taken in 1936, this view shows the pioneer diesel-electric locomotive operated by the B&O. The success of this locomotive was to encourage further dieselization on U.S. railroads, ultimately spelling the end of mainline steam. *Ian Allan Library*

LEFT: An Amtrak "SDP-40-F" locomotive pictured in the outskirts of Boston with a Boston-New York service in 1974. *Brian J. Cuddahy*

ABOVE: No. 200 was one of 25 600hp diesel-electric switchers built by EMD for the Baltimore & Ohio Railroad and placed into service in 1940. *B&OR*

LEFT: In May 1968 Burlington "E8" class No. 9940 departs from Chicago Union station with an evening commuter train. *R. K. Evans*

ABOVE: In April 1956 a diesel-hauled passenger service of the Atlantic Coast Line calls at Tampa, Florida. *B. A. Butt*

RIGHT: In April 1958, the southbound Daylight traverses a long series of level crossing as it approaches the station at Santa Barbara, California, behind two EMD-built diesel locomotives of the Southern Pacific. *B. A. Butt*

RIGHT: Two generations of Amtrak diesel stand alongside each other in June 1976: on the left is brand-new General Motors-built "F-40-PH" No. 200 while on the right stands one of the refurbished veteran Class E8 diesel-electrics, No. 283. *Brian J. Cudahy*

RIGHT: Constructed by GM between 1956 and 1960, the "FL9" was a passenger version of a predominantly freight model; two of the class, belonging to Penn Central, are seen at either end of the single-coach Dover Plains shuttle at Dover Plains. *Harry Luff Collection/Online Transport Archive*

RIGHT: Headed by an "E8" diesel, a Boston bound Amtrak train stops to pick up passengers at Kingston, Rhode Island, whilst a two-car RDC train waits on the opposite track. *Amtrak*

RIGHT: Southern Pacific No. 4374 was an EMD product of the mid-1950s of Class SD9; it was withdrawn before the SP and UP merged in 1996, although a number of the type did survive briefly in the expanded UP's ownership. *Harry Luff Collection/Online Transport Archive*

ABOVE: Two GNR "Z1" class electric locomotives, which usually worked together as semi-permanently coupled units generating some 4,330 hp, are seen hauling a passenger train. The class was introduced in the 1920s when the electrification of the route was upgraded to 11.5 kV. The Great Northern originally electrified its line through the Cascade Tunnels from 1909 onward; however, electric services were discontinued in 1956 when the line was converted to diesel-electric operation. *Ian Allan Library*

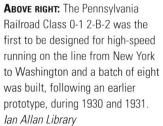

ABOVE RIGHT: The Pennsylvania Railroad Class 0-1 2-B-2 was the first to be designed for high-speed running on the line from New York to Washington and a batch of eight was built, following an earlier prototype, during 1930 and 1931. *Ian Allan Library*

RIGHT: Another line converted to electric traction was the Chicago, Milwaukee, St Paul, & Pacific Railroad, which began converting its 900-mile route from St Paul to Seattle in 1914. Using hydroelectric power and massive bipolar locomotives — nicknamed "Little Joes" (after Joseph Stalin because the locomotives were embargoed before export to the U.S.S.R.) — this was another line that succumbed to diesel traction after World War II. Pictured here is Chicago, Milwaukee, St Paul, & Pacific Railroad bipolar electric locomotive No. 10252. *Ian Allan Library*

RIGHT: New Haven Railroad No. 370, an "EP-5" class locomotive, pictured at Bridgeport, Connecticut with a working from Boston to New York. *Brian J. Cudahy*

RIGHT: Constructed from 1975, the GE-built "E-60CP" class of electric locomotive was designed by Amtrak to replace the "GG1s". At 6,000 hp, they were the most powerful locomotives in the United States at that time, but they failed to be reliable at the speeds intended — 125 mph — and Amtrak looked to France for its next generation of electric locomotive. *Harry Luff Collection/Online Transport Archive*

FAR RIGHT: One of the classic designs of locomotive operated by the "Pennsy" was the "GG1"—an electric class first introduced in 1935 as a joint venture between the railroad and Westinghouse. The last examples of the streamlined class were not withdrawn until 1983 and were the last Raymond Loewy-designed railroad equipment to operate. Here on June 13, 1942, No. 4857 is pictured at the head of the "Broadway Limited." *R. T. Dooner*

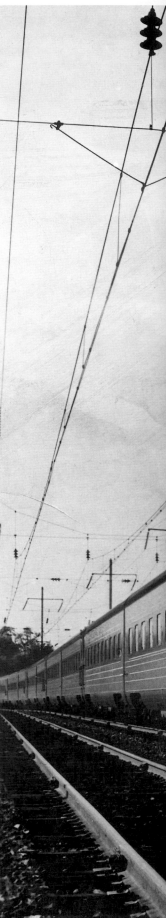

"*Acela Express trains are the only true high-speed train sets in the United States.*"
Wikipedia

ABOVE: Constructed by General Electric, No. 7809, one of the "L5" class, was supplied to the Pennsylvania Railroad in the early 1920s. Built to operate over lines electrified with a third rail, the locomotives were also fitted with pantographs to operate over those sections where overhead was installed. *GE*

RIGHT: An Amtrak express, formed of "Acela" unit No. 2037, pictured at South Norwalk, Connecticut, on November 3, 2002. *Brian Solomon*

RAILCARS

ABOVE: This two-car diesel railcar was constructed for the New York, Susquehanna, & Western Railroad by the American Car & Foundry Co.
Ian Allan Library

As the finances of the railway industry deteriorated, there were efforts to improve the economics of local services. Operators tried to make passenger trains more cost effective, and in 1949, for example, the Budd company launched its Rail Diesel Car (RDC). These vehicles, nicknamed "Doodlebugs," were designed to operate either singly or in multiple and undoubtedly the large numbers acquired after 1949 did help sustain many routes for longer than they would have done otherwise.

ABOVE: Railcars could be powered by steam, diesel, or electric traction; this two-car steam-powered railcar was delivered to the New Haven Railroad in the late 1930s. *Ian Allan Library*

LEFT: Louisville & Nashville Railroad No. 3600 was a 290 hp gas-electric motor car supplied to the railroad by General Electric. *Ian Allan Library*

LEFT: Railcar M100 preserved on the California Western Railroad of Fort Bragg, California. This railcar was restored after an accident in September 1964 in which the line's original railcar — M80 — was destroyed. *Harry Luff Collection/ Online Transport Archive*

RIGHT: The diesel-powered Rail Diesel Car produced by Budd was designed for low-cost passenger services; this example was delivered to the New York, New Haven, & Hartford Railroad. *Harry Luff Collection/Online Transport Archive*

BELOW: The California Western Railroad acquired the nickname "the Skunk Line" — which its current owners use for marketing the line today — as a result of the introduction of gas-powered railcars in the 1920s. The line still possesses a number of railcars, such as this Budd-built example, No. M300, seen at Fort Bragg. *Harry Luff Collection/Online Transport Archive*

RIGHT: An early 1960s view sees a Santa Fe diesel locomotive departing from Chicago with a passenger train; at this date long-distance passenger services remained in the hands of the traditional carriers. By the end of the decade, economics decreed that such services were no longer viable and Amtrak took over. *Harry Luff Collection/Online Transport Archive*

BELOW: Although the railroad companies had transferred their long-distance passenger services to Amtrak in the early 1970s, many continued to operate commuter services. One such was the Chicago & North Western; one of the railroad's double-deck units is pictured arriving into Chicago. *P. J. Howard*

FAR RIGHT: The Southern Railroad was one of three railroads to operate passenger services outside Amtrak after the nationalized system was created in 1971, although it was subsequently to join up. Here, in 1972, an Atlanta-Washington working is seen pulling into Washington Union. *Brian J. Cudahy*

HEAVY FREIGHT

With the gradual elimination of most of the long-distance passenger services or their transfer to Amtrak, the major U.S. railroad businesses are now almost exclusively freight only. Freight, however, has always been a diving force for the construction and opening of lines, with a large number of routes built that never saw passenger services.

"Handling freight as Freight Never Before was Handled."
CMStP&PR **c1910**

LEFT: In April 1956, on the Atlantic Coast Line, a freight train headed by two diesel locomotives traverses one of the main streets in Tampa, Florida, en route for Port Tampa.
B. A. Butt

RIGHT: The vast area of land occupied by the freight yards of the railroads is all too evident in this view of the Galewood Yard of the Chicago, Milwaukee, St Pauls, & Pacific Railroad taken in April 1943. *Library of Congress*

BELOW: On April 18, 1993 an eastbound Southern Pacific freight is pictured at Pinole, California. *Brian Solomon*

LEFT: An eastbound Union Pacific stack train heads through Clover Creek Canyon, Richmond, Nevada, on March 3, 1997. *Brian Solomon*

FAR LEFT: SD45 No. 6593 of Wisconsin Central recorded at the head of an iron ore train at Byron, Wisconsin, on April 6, 1996. *Brian Solomon*

BELOW: A General Electric-built Dash 8-40B No. 4026 heads a freight on the New York, Susquehanna, & Western Railroad in 1990. *Brian Solomon*

ABOVE: One of Amtrak's turboliners, the *Empire State Express*, glides across the Mohawk River at Rotterdam Junction during its daily run from New York City to Niagara Falls. Other stops served by the service included Buffalo, Rochester, and Albany. *Amtrak*

RIGHT: Amtrak service #303 from Chicago to St Louis seen at Springfield, Illinois. *Harry Luff Collection/Online Transport Archive*

FAR RIGHT: An Amtrak dual-mode "Genesis" unit pictured at Albany Rensellaer station on February 20, 2003. *Brian Solomon*

RECREATING THE PAST

The first standard gauge preserved line in the world was the Strasburg Railroad in Pennsylvania. Freight only from 1920, the line was to close completely in 1958; however, having been purchased by Henry K. Long it was to reopen the following year and has now been carrying passengers as a tourist line for almost half a century. When the 41/2-mile long line was originally reopened it was as a freight line, with a limited passenger service, but while revenue on freight was below expectations, that on the passenger side was encouraging enough to suggest that the company should concentrate on this aspect. Where the Strasburg blazed a trail, other lines both in the U.S.A. and throughout the world have followed.

In many respects the Strasburg Railroad's preservation is very typical of North American preservation. Unlike Europe, where many preservation schemes were not developed from any particular commercial aspiration but from a desire to preserve something that was in danger of being lost, much of preservation in the U.S.A. is more oriented towards the commercial tourist market. While there are the more conventional museums — such as the Baltimore & Ohio Railroad Museum and the Smithsonian — these are atypical. Most European countries have state-

sponsored national railroad museums covering the entire country's railroad history, but there is nothing directly comparable in the U.S.A. Moreover, while the majority of preserved lines in Europe are staffed almost exclusively by volunteers with relatively few paid staff, in the U.S.A. the reverse is true.

As part of the tourist industry there is an undoubted element of showbusiness in many of the United States' "preserved" lines. A notable example of this is the 3-mile long Tweetsie Railroad, near Blowing Rock, North Carolina. Closer in concept to a theme park, in which trains are held up by "bandits" and attacked by "Indians," before returning passengers to Tweetsie Town, a faithful reconstruction of a late 19th century railroad town.

The strength of the preservation movement is that it is a nationwide phenomenon. There are examples of museums right across the country, from the Baltimore & Ohio Museum in Baltimore, to the California State Railroad Museum in Sacramento. There are also countless preserved lines, both standard and narrow gauge, offering tourists the opportunity of sampling railway travel as it existed in the past.

It's not just the preservationists that have realized that money can be made from the running of special

RIGHT: There were a number of lines — such as the Georgetown Loop, Colorado — that were originally built to service the tourist industry. The majority of these were to close as a result of commercial pressures, but more recently, a number have been revived in order to reduce the pressure caused by road transport. One of these is the Georgetown Loop on which No. 14 is pictured hauling a demonstration freight train. *Derek Huntriss*

ABOVE: A number of sections of the narrow-gauge lines of the erstwhile Denver & Rio Grande survive in preservation. Here a "K-36" No. 489 and "K-37" No. 497 2-8-2s of the Cumbres & Toltec line are seen pulling a demonstration freight train about two miles from Chama on October 5, 1993. *Derek Huntriss*

LEFT: A 1913 Swedish-built 4-6-0 pictured in operation on the Belfast & Moosehead Lake Railroad in August 1997. The locomotive was acquired in 1995, when the Swedish government decided to dispose of its strategic reserve of steam locomotives, and given the name *Spirit of Unity. Brian Solomon*

FAR LEFT: The second section of the ex-Denver &Rio Grande to survive is the Durango & Silverton. Here the second of the "K-36" class 2-8-2s, No. 471, departs with a service to Silverton. The 10 locomotives of the "K-36" class were built by the Baldwin Locomotive Works in 1925 and were the last narrow-gauge locomotives built for use in the U.S. *Derek Huntriss*

trains. Increasingly, the commercial companies themselves have come to the conclusion that a profit can be made by scheduling special trains aimed at tourists. In a sense, as the main railroad companies grasped that money can be made from these services, preservation has come full circle. Initially designed to try to secure historical items that were considered life-expired and unprofitable, the preservation of old lines and rolling stock is now considered an additional source of revenue by the major rail companies.

LEFT: Located in the mountains of West Virginia, the standard-gauge Cass Scenic Railroad operates over lines originally constructed for exploiting the area's forests. Following final closure, a preserved section first opened in 1963. No. 5, illustrated here, is one of a number of three-truck Shays to be based on the line. *Derek Huntriss*

BELOW LEFT: There are a large number of railroad museums within the U.S. that house both static and operational exhibits. These include Steamtown, which incorporates two original roundhouses on the site of the former Scranton yards of the Delaware, Lackawanna, & Western Railroad in Scranton, Pennsylvania. The collection's ex-Canadian National 2-8-2 No. 3254 is pictured in steam in August 2007. *Brian Solomons*

FAR LEFT: The East Broad Top Railroad in Pennsylvania was an unusual survivor in that it was and is owned by a scrapdealer who originally acquired the line in the late 1950s to dismantle it. In 1960, the local boroughs of Rockhill and Orbisonia celebrated their bicentenaries. To mark the event, the owner was asked to display a commemorative train. However, he decided to restore four miles of track and two locomotives, allowing operation over a few months. Such was the success that the service, now extended over five miles, was restored again in 1961 and it has been running each summer since then. Built by Baldwin in 1912, EBT No. 14 is pictured on October 11, 1997. *Brian Solomon*

OPPOSITE, ABOVE: The Valley Railway (Connecticut) operates over some 23 miles of former Penn Central track out of Essex, Connecticut. The locomotive is ex-Aberdeen & Rockfish 2-8-2 No. 40, originally built by Alco in 1920 and acquired by the A&RR in 1935. The Valley Railroad obtained it in 1977. *Brian Solomon*

OPPOSITE, BELOW: The Conway Scenic Railroad operates a number of excursion trains from its base at North Conway in New Hampshire using ex-Canadian National 7470. *Brian Solomon*

LEFT: Another exhibit at Steamtown is ex-Union Pacific "Big Boy" No. 4012. Although no fewer than eight of this class survive, there are also countless examples of classic designs that have not survived. Among the many losses are the streamlined "J3" class "Hudsons" of the New York Central, and the same company's iconic "Niagara" class 4-8-4s of 1945-46. *Derek Huntriss*

"The paramount historical significance of the first transcontinental railroad lies in its effect upon the Far Western frontier. It made the first serious breech in the frontier, and established the process by which the entire frontier was then to be demolished."

Robert M. Utley **1960**

FAR LEFT: The use of preserved steam locomotives on the main line has helped to recreate the long-lost era of the golden age of the railroad. Here Union Pacific No. 8444 hauls a special between Stirling and Denver. *Derek Huntriss*

CENTER LEFT: As generations move on, so does nostalgia and there are now significant numbers of railroad enthusiasts who only know diesel traction. As the first and second generation diesel locomotives succumbed, so a number have entered preservation. Here an example is seen in service on the Fillmore & Western Railway based at Fillmore, California, in May 2001. The railroad operates over part of the Southern Pacific Santa Paula branch line. *John Vaughan*

ABOVE LEFT: Not all preserved railroads survive. Casualties have occurred for a number of reasons — financial or physical, where, for example, flooding has caused the loss of the trackbed — and one such casualty was the West Side & Cherry Railroad in California. When originally closed the line was the last surviving narrow-gauge railroad in the west. WS&CR No. 15, pictured here, is now to be found on the Yosemite Mountain & Sugar Pine Railroad. *Harry Luff/Online Transport Archive*

LEFT: All that is "preserved" is not actually what it purports to be. In order to recreate the classic meeting at Promontory Summit, Utah, replicas of the two locomotives used originally — Union Pacific No. 119 (seen here) and Central Pacific No. 60 — have been built. *P. J. Howard*

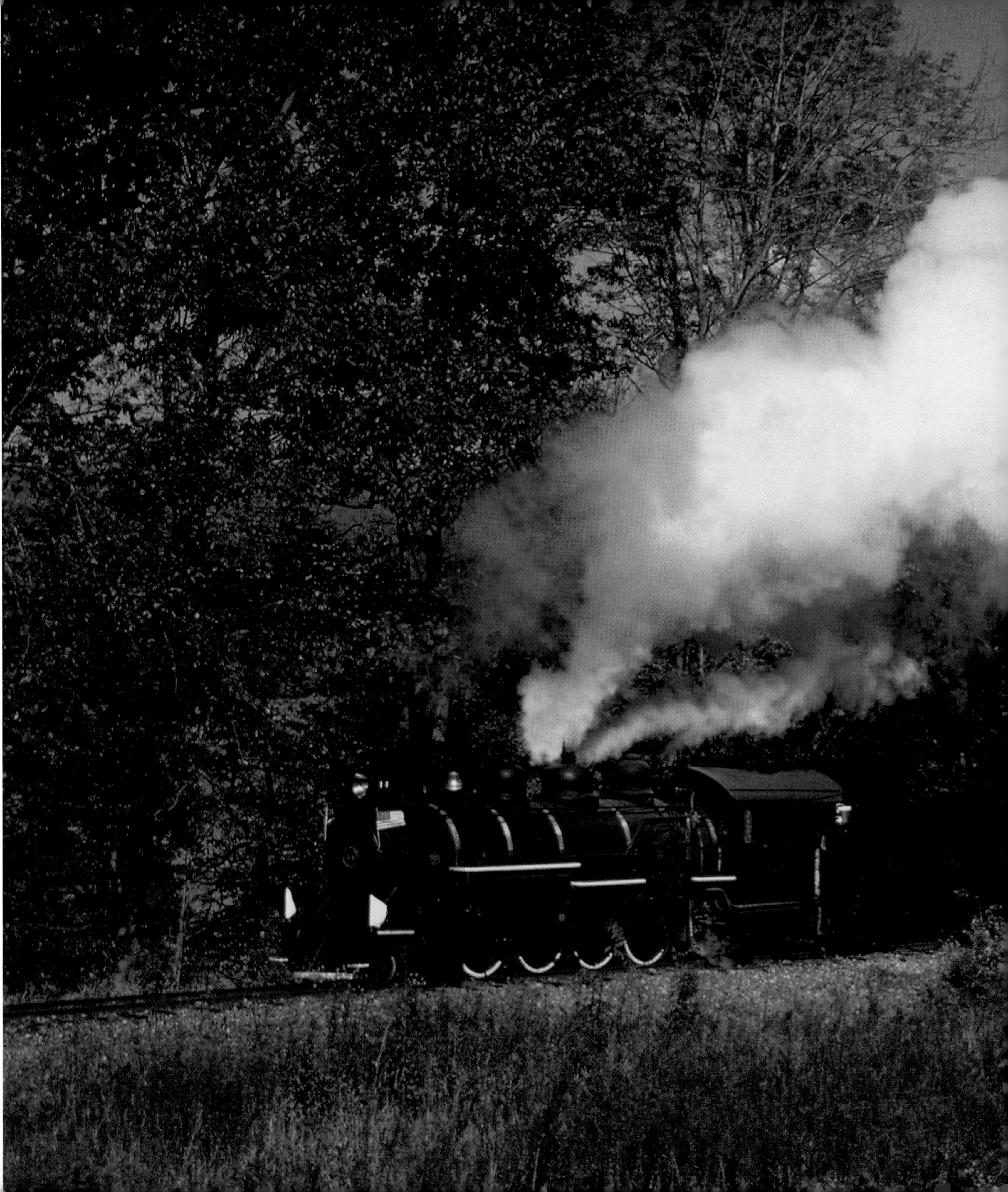

INDEX